Writing Literature Reviews

A Guide for Students of the Social and Behavioral Sciences

Jose L. Galvan

California State University, Los Angeles

Pyrczak Publishing
P.O. Box 39731 • Los Angeles, CA 90039

Editorial assistance provided by Brenda Koplin, Elaine Fuess, Sharon Young, and Cheryl Alcorn.

Cover design by Robert Kibler and Larry Nichols.

Printed in the United States of America.
10 9 8 7 6 5 4 3   DOC   06 05 04 03 02 01 00

ISBN 1-884585-18-3

Table of Contents

Detailed Table of Contents

Introduction

This book was written to help students understand the steps involved in preparing literature reviews in the social and behavioral sciences. The primary focus is on reviewing original research published in academic journals and on its relationship to theoretical literature. However, most of the guidelines presented here can also be applied to reviews of other kinds of source materials.

Audience for this Book

This book was written for students who are required to "do library research" and write literature reviews as term papers in content-area classes in the social and behavioral sciences. Often, their previous training has not prepared them to search databases for reports of original research and related theoretical literature, analyze these particular types of literature, and synthesize them into a cohesive narrative. Instead, they are often taught how to use secondary sources such as encyclopedias, reports in the mass media, and books that synthesize the work of others. In addition, they are usually not taught the conventions for writing papers in the social and behavioral sciences. This book is designed to fill this gap by giving students detailed, step-by-step guidance on how to write reviews of primary source materials.

Students who are beginning to work on their theses and dissertations will also benefit from this book if they have not previously received instruction in how to prepare critical analyses of published research and the theories on which it is based. Undertaking a thesis or dissertation is stressful. This book should serve as a source of calm and logic as they begin to work on their literature review chapter.

Finally, those who are preparing to write literature reviews for possible publication in journals as well as those who need to include literature reviews in grant proposals will find many portions of this book helpful.

Unique Features

The following features make this book unique among textbooks designed to teach analytical writing.
- The book's focus is on writing critical reviews of original research.
- It guides students through a systematic, multistep writing process.
- The steps and guidelines are organized sequentially and illustrated with examples from a wide range of academic journals.
- Each chapter is designed to help students develop a set of specific products that will contribute toward a competent literature review.

Notes to the Instructor

Many colleges and universities have adopted a "writing-across-the-curriculum" program, in which all students are required to write papers in all courses. While the goals of such a program are admirable, many instructors are pressed for time to cover just the traditional content of their courses and have little time to teach writing. Such instructors will find this book useful because the explicit steps in the writing process illustrated with examples throughout this book make it possible for students to use it largely on their own. In addition, many professors "naturally" write well, but have given little thought and have no training in *how to teach writing*. Used as a supplement, this book solves that dilemma by providing a detailed guide to the writing process.

Much of what most of us know about writing was learned through what Kamhi-Stein (1997) calls the "one-shot writing assignment" (p. 52).[1] This is where the instructor gives an assignment at the beginning of the term, using the writing prompt, "Write a paper about *<specific topic>*." Conceptually, we tend to view this type of assignment as a single task, even though we may go through several discrete steps in the process of completing it. In fact, when writing papers that involve library research, the quality of the finished product depends in large measure on the care with which we undertake each of these steps.

In this book, the activities at the end of each chapter are designed to guide students through these various steps or stages of the writing process. These activities can be recast as a series of tasks that can easily be incorporated into the syllabus of a survey course in a specific discipline, as a multi-step writing assignment. Thus, this book has two complementary audiences: (a) instructors who may want to incorporate this multi-step writing approach into their course syllabus and (b) students, working independently, who may need help in planning and implementing the various stages involved in completing a major writing assignment such as the literature review chapter of a thesis or dissertation.

Acknowledgments

Over the past several years, I have watched with delight as my daughter, Melisa, blossomed into the wonderfully creative and independent writer that she is today, and it is with great pride and deep gratitude that I acknowledge her assistance with this book. Her help in ensuring the accuracy of the citations and references saved me some valuable time, but more important, it made me realize in a personal way the benefits that can come from role modeling. I also appreciate the patience and cooperation of Jim Rodacker and Janine Galvan for being willing to adjust schedules (often at the last minute) and tolerate a totally self-absorbed and driven writer for the extended period that it took to write this book. I also thank my supervisor, Dr. Theodore J. Crovello, for allowing me to schedule days off when I needed them and for encouraging me to find ways to continue to pursue my professional and academic interests, even while working as an administrator.

I am indebted to my editor, Dr. Fred Pyrczak, for suggesting the topic for this book and for his generous assistance with the research design content of Chapters 1 and 5. I am also indebted to my colleagues on the faculty of California State University, Los Angeles, especially Drs. Marguerite Ann Snow and Lia D. Kamhi-Stein, whose work on the multistep writing approach inspired the book's organization.[2] All three of these individuals offered countless helpful suggestions, most of which are now part of the final manuscript. Errors and omissions, of course, remain my responsibility.

Jose L. Galvan
Los Angeles, California

---

[1] Kamhi-Stein, L. D. (1997). Redesigning the writing assignment in general education courses. *College ESL, 7*(1), 49-61.

[2] Dr. Marguerite Ann Snow was director of Project LEAP: Learning-English-for-Academic-Purposes. This was a curricular reform project at California State University, Los Angeles, funded by a grant from the Fund for the Improvement of Postsecondary Education (FIPSE), 1991-1997. For more information about this project, see Snow, M. A. (1994). *Project LEAP training manual. Year three.* Los Angeles: Fund for the Improvement of Postsecondary Education and California State University, Los Angeles, and Snow, M. A. & Kamhi-Stein, L. D. (Eds.), *Teaching academic literacy skills: Strategies for content faculty.* Los Angeles: Fund for the Improvement of Postsecondary Education and California State University, Los Angeles.

Notes

Chapter 1

An Introduction to Writing Reviews of Academic Literature

In this book, you will be learning how to write a review of the literature using primary (original) sources of information in the social and behavioral sciences. By far, the most common primary sources are reports of empirical research published in academic journals. This chapter begins with a brief overview of this type of source. It is followed by brief descriptions of four other types of literature found in journals: theoretical articles, review articles, anecdotal reports, and reports on professional practices and standards. This is followed by a brief discussion of the writing process you will be using as you write your review. This discussion also serves as an overview of the rest of the book, which was designed as a guide for students who are new to the specialized requirements of writing a literature review in the social and behavioral sciences.

An Introduction to Reviewing Primary Sources

Why Focus on Empirical Research Reports?

The focus of this book is on *original* reports of research found in academic journals. They are *original* because they are the first published accounts of the research. As such, they are *primary sources* of information, providing detailed reports on the methodology used in the research and detailed descriptions and discussions of the findings. In contrast, research summaries reported in textbooks, popular magazines, and newspapers as well as on television and radio are usually *secondary sources*, which often provide only global descriptions of results with few details on the methodology used to obtain them. As scholars, you will want to emphasize primary sources when you review the literature on a particular topic. In fact, your instructor may require you to cite these sources exclusively in your written reviews of literature.

Journals in the social and behavioral sciences abound with original reports of *empirical research*. The term *empirical* refers to *observation* while the term *empirical research* refers to *systematic observation*. Research is systematic because researchers plan in advance whom to observe, for what characteristics to observe, how to observe, and so on. While such research is the foundation of any science, one could reasonably argue that all empirical research is inherently flawed and, hence, the results obtained with research should be interpreted with caution. For example, listed below are three major problematic issues that arise in almost all empirical studies and the problems they pose for students who review them.

- *Issue 1: Sampling.* Most researchers study only a sample and infer that the results apply to some larger group (often called the population). Furthermore, most use samples with some kind of bias that makes them unrepresentative of the populations of interest.[1] For instance, suppose a professor conducted research using only students in his or her introductory psychology class or suppose a researcher mailed a questionnaire and obtained only a 40% return. Clearly, these samples might not be representative of the populations of interest.

  > Problem: A reviewer needs to consider sampling bias, if there is any, in interpreting the results of a study. Deciding how much trust to put in the results of a study based on a biased sample is a highly subjective judgment.

- *Issue 2: Measurement.* Almost all instruments used for measurement in empirical research should be presumed to be flawed to some extent. For example, suppose a researcher uses a self-report questionnaire to measure the incidence of marijuana use on a campus. Even if respondents are assured that their responses are confidential and anonymous, some might not want to reveal their illegal behavior. On the other hand, others might be tempted to brag about doing something illegal even if they seldom or never do it. So what are the alternatives? One is to conduct personal interviews, but this measurement technique also calls for revelation of an illegal activity. Another alternative is a covert observation, but this technique might be unethical. On the other hand, if the observation is not covert, participants might change their behavior because they know they are being observed. As you can see, there is no perfect solution.

  > Problem: A reviewer needs to consider the possibilities for error in measurement. Ask yourself whether the method of measurement seems sound. Did the researcher use more than one method of measurement? If so, do the various methods yield consistent results?

- *Issue 3: Problem identification.* Researchers usually examine only a piece of a problem—often just a very small piece. Here is an example: Suppose a researcher wants to study the use of rewards in the classroom and its effects on creativity. At first, this sounds manageable as a research problem until one considers that there are many kinds of rewards—many kinds and levels of praise, many types of prized objects that might be given, and so on. Another issue is that there are many different ways in which creativity can be expressed. For example, creativity is expressed differently in the visual arts, in dance, and in music. Additional forms of creativity can be expressed in the

---

[1] If you have taken a course in research methods or statistics, you know that random sampling (like drawing names out of a hat) is preferred over biased sampling. Note, however, that random sampling introduces chance errors, which can be assessed with inferential statistics, a topic that is beyond the scope of this book.

physical sciences, in oral expression, written communication, and so on. No researcher has the resources to examine all of these. Instead, he or she will probably have to select one or two types of rewards and one or two manifestations of creativity and examine them in a limited number of classrooms.

Problem: A reviewer needs to synthesize the various research reports on narrowly defined problems in a given area, looking for consistencies and discrepancies from report to report while keeping in mind that each researcher defined his or her problem in a somewhat different way from the others. Due to the fact that empirical research provides only approximations and degrees of evidence on research problems that are necessarily limited in scope, creating a synthesis is like trying to put together a jigsaw puzzle, knowing in advance that most of the pieces are missing and that many of the available pieces are not fully formed.

Considering the three issues presented above, you might be tempted to conclude that reviewing original reports of empirical research is difficult. Undoubtedly, it sometimes is. However, if you pick a topic of interest to you and thoroughly read the research on that topic, you will soon become immersed in a fascinating project. On the vast majority of topics in the social and behavioral sciences, there are at least minor disagreements about the interpretation of the available research data and, often, major disagreements. Hence, you may soon find yourself acting like a juror, deliberating about which researchers seem to have the most cohesive and logical arguments, which ones have the strongest evidence and so on. .

You might also incorrectly conclude that only students who have intensively studied research methods and statistics can make sense of original research reports. While such a background undoubtedly is helpful, this book was written with the assumption that any intelligent, careful reader can make sense out of a body of empirical research if he or she reads carefully and extensively on the topic selected for review. Authors of reports of original research do not just present statistics in isolation. Instead, they usually provide definitions of basic concepts, discuss their theoretical orientations, describe their reasoning for approaching their research in the way they did, and offer interpretations moderated by discussions of the limitations of their methodology. In fact, it is common for these writers to provide separate sections, usually near the end of their reports, in which they pause to discuss the methodological limitations of their studies and the implications of the limitations for interpreting their results. In other words, a skilled author of a report on original empirical research will guide you through the material even if you do not understand all the research jargon and statistics.

One final consideration: It is essential that you carefully and thoroughly read all the research articles that you cite. Reading only the brief abstracts (summaries) at the beginning of such articles may mislead you because of the lack of detail and, therefore, cause you to mislead the readers of your literature review. Thus, it is your ethical responsibility to read each cited reference in its entirety.

Another Kind of Primary Source: Theoretical Articles

Not every journal article is a report of original research. In fact, some articles are written for the explicit purpose of evaluating an existing theory or to propose a new one. Remember, a *theory* is a general explanation of why variables work together, how they are related to each other, and especially, how they influence each other. As a unifying construct, a theory helps to explain how seemingly unrelated empirical observations tie together and make sense. Here is a brief example:

> Weiss (1975) proposed a *relational theory of loneliness*. Among other things, this theory distinguishes between *emotional loneliness* (utter loneliness created by the lack of a close emotional attachment to another person) and *social loneliness* (feelings of isolation and loneliness created by the absence of a close social network). This theory has important implications for many areas of social and behavioral research. For example, if the theory is correct, it would predict that someone who is in bereavement due to the death of a spouse with whom they had a close emotional attachment will experience utter loneliness that cannot be moderated through mere social support. [2]

Notice two things about the example given above. First, the prediction based on the theory runs counter to this common sense notion: that those who are lonely due to the loss of a significant other will feel less lonely with the social support of family and friends. The theory suggests that this notion is only partially true at best. Specifically, it suggests that family and friends will be able to lessen only *social loneliness* but be ineffective in lessening the more deeply felt and potentially devastating *emotional loneliness*. Note that it is not uncommon for a theory to lead to predictions that run counter to common sense. In fact, this is a hallmark of theories that make important contributions to understanding human affairs and our physical world.

Second, Weiss' theory can be tested with empirical research. A researcher can study those who have lost significant others, asking them about how lonely they feel and the types and strength of support they receive. To be useful, a theory should be testable with empirical methods, which helps the scientific community determine the extent of its validity.

---

[2] This example is based on material in Stroebe, W., Stroebe, M., Abakoumkin, G., & Schut, H. (1996). The role of loneliness and social support in adjustment to loss: A test of attachment versus Stress Theory. *Journal of Personality and Social Psychology, 70*, 1241-1249. Also, see Weiss, R.S. (1975). *Loneliness: The experience of emotional and social isolation*. Cambridge, MA: MIT Press.

Your job in reviewing literature will be made easier if you identify the major theories that apply to your topic of interest. Writers of empirical research reports often identify underlying theories and discuss whether their results are consistent with them. Following up on the leads they give you in their references to the theoretical literature will provide you with a framework for thinking about the bits and pieces of evidence you find in various reports about specific, usually narrow, research projects that are published in academic journals. In fact, you might choose to build your literature review around one or more theories.

It is important to note that a literature review that contributes to a better understanding of one or more theories has the potential to make an important contribution to the writer's field because theories often have broad implications for many areas of concern in human affairs.

Literature Review Articles

Journals often carry literature review articles,[3] that is, articles that review the literature on a specific topic—much like the literature review that you will be writing while using this book. Most journals that publish review articles set a relatively high standard for accepting such articles. Not only should they be well-written analytical narratives that bring readers up to date on what is known about a given topic, but they should also provide fresh insights that advance knowledge. These insights may take many forms. Some major ones are: resolving conflicts among studies that previously seemed to contradict each other, identifying new ways to interpret research results on a topic, and laying out a path for future research that has the potential to advance the field significantly. As a result, going through the steps of preparing a literature review is not an easy way to get published in a journal. In fact, when you begin reviewing the literature on a topic, there is no guarantee that you will arrive at the level of insight that will pass the scrutiny of a journal's editorial board. However, if you follow the guidelines outlined in this book, which emphasize analyzing literature (casting a critical eye on it; pulling it apart, sometimes into pieces and bits; and putting them back together in a new form), you stand a better chance than the average academic writer of producing a review suitable for publication.

It is worth noting that sometimes students are discouraged when they find that their topic has recently been reviewed in an academic journal. They may feel that if it was already reviewed, they should select a different topic. This is not necessarily a wise decision. Instead, these students usually should feel fortunate to have the advantage of someone else's labor and insights—someone that can be cited, someone on whose work they can build or with whom they can agree or disagree. Writing is an individual process, so two people reviewing the same body

---

[3] Some journals also carry book reviews, test reviews, and reviews of other products and services. These will not be considered in this book. Hence, the term "review article" in this book refers only to a *literature review article*.

of literature are likely to produce distinctly different, but potentially equally worthy reviews.[4]

Anecdotal Reports

As you review the literature on a specific topic, you may encounter articles that are built on anecdotal accounts of personal experiences. An anecdote is a description of an experience that happened to be noticed (as opposed to an observation that is based on research, in which there was considerable planning regarding whom and what to observe as well as when to observe a particular phenomenon in order to gather the best information). Anecdotal accounts are most common in journals aimed at practicing professionals such as clinical psychologists, social workers, and teachers. For example, a teacher might write a journal article describing his or her experiences with a severely underachieving student who bloomed academically while in his or her classroom. Other teachers may find this interesting and worth reading as a source of potential ideas, but as a contribution to science, such anecdotes are seriously deficient. Without control and comparison, we do not know to what extent this teacher has contributed to the student's progress, if at all. Perhaps the student would have bloomed without the teacher's efforts because of improved conditions at home or because of a prescription drug for hyperactivity prescribed by a physician without the teacher's knowledge. Given these limitations, anecdotal reports should be used very sparingly in literature reviews, and when they are cited, they should be clearly labeled as being anecdotal.

Reports on Professional Practices and Standards

Some journals aimed at practicing professionals publish reports on practices and standards such as newly adopted curriculum standards for mathematics instruction in a state, or proposed legislation to allow clinical psychologists to prescribe prescription drugs. When these types of issues are relevant to a topic being reviewed, they often merit discussion in a literature review.

The Writing Process

Now that we have considered the major types of materials you will be reviewing (reports of empirical research, theoretical articles, literature review articles, articles based on anecdotal evidence, and reports on professional practices and standards), we will briefly consider the process you will follow in this book.

An important, and often overlooked, distinction is made in this book between *conducting* a literature review (i.e., locating literature, reading it, and

---

[4] Keep in mind that empirical knowledge is an ever-evolving process—not a set of facts. Nothing is proven by empirical research; rather, we use research to arrive at varying degrees of confidence. Thus, researchers may differ in their *interpretations* even if they review the same literature.

mentally analyzing it) and *writing* a literature review. Needless to say, one needs to first locate, read, and analyze literature before a review can be written. Furthermore, writing a literature review involves a series of steps. In the field of composition and rhetoric, these steps collectively are referred to as the writing process. They include planning, organizing, drafting, editing, and redrafting. More specifically, the process involves defining a topic and selecting the literature for review (planning); analyzing, synthesizing, and evaluating the articles being reviewed (organizing); writing a first draft of the review (drafting); checking the draft for completeness, cohesion, and correctness (editing); and rewriting the draft (redrafting). The process is much like the one you may have followed in your freshman English class when you were asked to write an analytical essay. The organization of this book follows these steps in the writing process.

Writing for a Specific Purpose

The first order of business is to consider your reasons for writing a literature review. Reviews of empirical research can serve several purposes. They can constitute the essence of a research paper in a class, which can vary in length and complexity depending on the professor's criteria for the paper. In a journal article, the literature review is often brief and to the point, usually focusing on providing the rationale for specific research questions. In contrast, the literature review in a thesis or dissertation is usually meant to establish that the writer has a thorough command of the literature on the topic being studied. Obviously, these different purposes will result in literature reviews that vary in length and style. Chapter 2, *Considerations in Writing Reviews for Specific Purposes*, describes the differences in these three kinds of reviews.

Planning to Write

The first two tasks in planning to write a review of empirical research are defining the topic and locating relevant research articles. These steps are interrelated—the topic you specify will determine the specific literature you identify, and oftentimes the results of your literature search will guide you in defining the topic. Sometimes your instructor will assign a specific topic for a term paper; other times, the choice will be left up to you. The process of defining the topic is the first step covered in Chapter 3, *Selecting a Topic and Identifying Literature for Review*.

The remainder of Chapter 3 deals with the process of *selecting relevant journal articles*. Research libraries are not what they used to be. While searching the library's stacks may prove fruitful for you, it can be a hit-or-miss experience because a library's holdings will vary greatly depending on resources, availability, and even vandalism. A better option is to search the available databases and World Wide Web resources. Reference librarians can help you get started, or you can sign up for a workshop on how to use new electronic resources. This book is designed to teach you some of the basic steps involved in searching databases. However, keep in mind that each database has its own unique features. It is beyond the scope of this book to describe these differences in detail.

Once you have located an adequate collection of articles concerning your topic, you should read and analyze them. This step is called the *analysis*—this involves reading an article and taking notes. In other words, as you read, you separate the author's prose into its parts or elements. Because you will be analyzing a number of articles, you will need to prepare a systematic collection of notes. Part of the analysis process is sifting the elements on which you made notes, retaining the pertinent ones, and discarding those you do not need. This step is the subject of Chapter 4, *General Guidelines for Analyzing Literature*.

It is sometimes necessary to read and analyze the literature from a more specialized perspective. For example, if your literature review is part of a research study you are planning to conduct, either in preparing to write a thesis or dissertation or in writing an article intended for publication in a journal, you will want to pay special attention to Chapter 5, *Analyzing Literature from the Viewpoint of a Researcher*, which provides a brief overview of more technical issues.

Organizing Your Notes and Your Thoughts

Having followed the above steps, you should begin creating a synthesis, which involves putting the parts from your notes back together into a new whole. Think of it like this: Each of the articles you have read constitutes its own whole; in your research notes, you have written down parts or elements from each article; now, you should put these notes back together in the form of a new organizational framework. Once you have created the new framework, you should evaluate the contents. In other words, you now need to describe your evaluation of the quality and importance of the research you have cited. These steps are covered in Chapter 6, *Synthesizing Literature Prior to Writing a Review*.

Drafting, Editing, and Redrafting

Next, you should write your first draft. Based on your audience, you should decide whether you will write in a formal or less formal *voice*. An effective writer is aware of the reader's expectations. A term paper written for a professor who is knowledgeable in a particular field is different from a literature review in a thesis, which may be read by readers who are curious, but not necessarily knowledgeable, about a topic. A literature review in a thesis is different from a literature review in an article intended for publication in a journal or in a paper for a class. You should also identify the major subtopics and determine the patterns that have emerged from your notes, such as trends, similarities, contrasts, and generalizations. These steps are covered in Chapter 7, *Guidelines for Writing a First Draft*.

Next, you should make sure that your argument is clear, logical, and well supported, and that your draft is free of errors. Chapter 8, *Guidelines for Developing a Coherent Essay*, will help you make sure that your argument makes sense to you and your reader. Chapter 9, *Guidelines on Style, Mechanics, and Language Usage*, describes the first steps in making sure that your review is free of errors.

The final two chapters of the book coincide with the last two steps in the writing process: editing and redrafting. These steps are iterative, that is, they are meant to be repeated. It is not uncommon for a professional writer to rewrite five or more drafts, each time producing a refined new draft. Chapter 10, *Incorporating Feedback and Refining the First Draft*, provides guidelines on how to approach this stage in the writing process. Finally, Chapter 11, *Comprehensive Self-editing Checklist for Refining the Final Draft*, gives a detailed checklist for use in editing your own manuscript for style and correctness. Formal academic writing requires that you prepare a manuscript as free of errors as possible, and this checklist will help you accomplish this goal.

Activities for Chapter 1

1. Locate an original report of empirical research in your field, read it, and respond to the following questions. (How to locate journal articles on specific topics is covered in considerable detail later in this book. At this point, simply locate one in your general field of study. Your reference librarian or instructor can help you identify specific journals in your field that are available in your college library. Scan the tables of contents for a research article on a topic of interest and make a photocopy to bring to class with your answers.) Note that your instructor may want to assign a particular article for this activity.

   A. Are there any obvious sampling problems? Explain. (Do not just read the section under the subheading "sample" because researchers sometimes provide additional information about the sample throughout their reports, especially in the introduction where they might point out how their sample is different from those used by other researchers or near the end where they might discuss the limitations of the sample in relation to the results.)

   B. Are there any obvious measurement problems? Explain.

C. Has the researcher examined only a narrowly defined problem? Is it too narrow? Explain.

D. Did you notice any other flaws? Explain.

E. Overall, do you think that the research makes an important contribution to advancing knowledge? Explain.

2. Read Review Article A in the Supplementary Readings section at the end of this book and respond to the following questions. (Note that you will want to read this review again after you have learned more about the process of writing a literature review. The questions below ask only for your first, general impressions. Later, you will be able to critique it in more detail.)

A. Have the reviewers clearly identified the topic of the review? Have they indicated its delimitations (e.g., Is it limited to a certain period of time? Does it deal with only certain aspects of the problem?)

B. Have the reviewers written a cohesive essay that guides you through the literature from subtopic to subtopic? Explain.

C. Have the reviewers *interpreted* the literature (as opposed to merely summarizing it)? Explain.

D. Overall, do you think the reviewers make an important contribution to knowledge? Explain.

Chapter 2

Considerations in Writing Reviews for Specific Purposes

Although the guidelines given in this book apply to any literature review, you will want to vary your approach to the writing task depending on your purpose for writing your review. This chapter focuses on the three most common purposes for writing a critical review of research and the audience for each type: writing a literature review as a term paper for a class, as a chapter for a thesis or dissertation, and as part of an introduction to a journal article.

Writing a Literature Review as a Term Paper for a Class

Writing a literature review as a term paper assignment for a class can be somewhat frustrating because the task involves (a) selecting a topic in a field that may be new to you, (b) identifying and locating an appropriate number of research articles using databases and journals that you may not be familiar with, and (c) writing and editing a well-developed essay, all in about two to three months. To compound matters, most instructors will expect you to prepare your review of literature on your own outside of class with minimal guidance from them. Still, they expect that your literature review will be thoroughly researched and well written. This book will help you accomplish this.

With these difficulties in mind, it is necessary for you to plan your term paper project carefully. First, you should make sure you understand the assignment and know as much as possible about your instructor's expectations near the beginning of the semester. Thus, you should not hesitate to raise questions in class regarding the assignment. Keep in mind that if something is not clear to you, it may be unclear to other students who will benefit by hearing the answers to your questions.[1] Second, you will have to pace yourself as you undertake the writing process. Make sure that you allow sufficient time to follow the steps outlined in this book, including selecting a topic, reading and evaluating the relevant research articles, synthesizing and organizing your notes, writing, revising, and redrafting your paper, and editing it for correctness and adherence to

---

[1] Idiosyncratic questions that other students may not find of interest generally should be raised with the instructor outside of class, perhaps during office hours. Examples are: You are planning to go to graduate school and want to write a more extensive paper than required by the professor. You have written a literature review for a previous class and would prefer to expand on it rather than write a new review.

the required style manual. It is helpful to map out the weeks of your school term and lay out a timeline. The following is a suggested timeline for a 15-week semester.

Example 2.1

Stage 1.   Preliminary library search and selection of topic
             Complete by the end of Week 3
Stage 2.   Reading list and preliminary paper outline
             Complete by the end of Week 6
Stage 3.   First draft of paper
             Complete by the end of Week 12
Stage 4.   Revised final draft of paper
             Complete by the end of Week 15

Individual instructors' expectations regarding length of a written review and the number of references cited may vary widely. For term papers written for introductory survey courses, instructors may require only a short review—perhaps as short as a few double-spaced, typewritten pages with a minimum of five to ten references. For such a review, you will need to be highly selective in identifying and citing references—usually selecting those that are the most important and/or most current. For upper-division courses, instructors may require longer reviews with more references. Finally, for graduate-level classes in your academic major, your instructor may place no restrictions on length or number of references, expecting you to review as many research reports as needed to write a comprehensive literature review on your topic.

Given the limited time frame for writing a term paper, your topic should usually be kept narrow. Look for an area that is well defined, especially if you are new to a field. A good way to select a topic is to examine the subheadings within the chapters in your textbook. For example, an educational psychology textbook might have a chapter on creativity with subsections on definitions of creativity, the measurement of creativity, and fostering creativity in the classroom. As an example, suppose you are especially interested in fostering creativity in the classroom. Reading this section, you might find that your textbook author mentions that there is some controversy on the effects of competition on promoting creativity (i.e., can teachers foster creativity by offering rewards for its expression?). This sounds like a fairly narrow topic that you might start with as a tentative topic. As you search for journal articles on this topic,[2] you may find that

---

[2] Searching electronic databases with an emphasis on how to narrow the search is discussed in detail in the next chapter.

there are more articles on it than you need for the term project assignment. If so, you can narrow the topic further by specifying that your review will deal with competition and creativity only in (a) elementary school samples and (b) the fine arts.

If you are not given a choice of topics and are assigned a topic by your instructor, begin your search for literature as soon as possible and report to him or her any difficulties you encounter such as finding that there is too little research on the assigned topic (perhaps the topic can be broadened or your instructor can point you to additional sources your search did not identify) or there is too much research (perhaps the topic can be narrowed or your instructor can help you identify other delimiters such as reviewing only recent articles).

One of the consequences of having a short time frame for preparing a term paper is that opportunities for feedback on your early drafts will be limited, so you will be responsible for doing much of the editing yourself. When you lay out your timeline, try to leave time to consult with your instructor about your first draft, even if this has to be done during an office visit. It sometimes helps students to be able to see an example of an acceptable term paper written by a student in a previous term. Many instructors will permit you to review sample papers. Finally, you should use the self-editing guide at the end of this book to help you eliminate some common problems before you turn in your paper.

Writing a Literature Review Chapter for a Thesis or Dissertation

The review chapter for a thesis or dissertation is the most complex of the literature review types covered in this book because you will be expected to prepare the initial literature review as part of your research proposal, well before you begin your actual research. Conducting a literature review is one of the steps you will follow in the process of defining the research questions for your study, so you will probably have to redefine your topic and revise your research questions several times along the way.

Students writing a literature review chapter frequently ask, "How many articles must I read?" In addition, they ask, "How long should I make the review?" Students often are frustrated when they hear that there are no preset minimums either on the number of research articles to review or on the length of a review chapter.

You should establish two main goals for your literature review. First, attempt to provide a *comprehensive* and *up-to-date* review of the topic. Second, try to demonstrate that you have a thorough command of the field you are studying. Keep in mind that the literature review will provide the basic rationale for your research, and the extent to which you accomplish these goals will contribute in large measure to how well your project will be received. Note that these goals reflect the seriousness of the task you have undertaken, which is to contribute to the body of knowledge in your field. Several traditions that have evolved through the years reflect how seriously academic departments view the writing of a thesis or dissertation. They include the defense of the research proposal, the defense of the finished thesis or dissertation, and the careful scrutiny given the final document by the university's librarian prior to its acceptance as a permanent addition to the library's holdings.

Some students procrastinate when it comes to writing a literature review chapter. After all, there are no set timelines. Therefore, it is important for you to set deadlines for yourself. Some students find it useful to plan an informal timeline in collaboration with the committee chair, perhaps by setting deadlines for completing the various steps involved in the overall process. The guidelines described in this book will be helpful in this regard. You should adopt a regular pattern of consulting with the professors on your committee to ensure that you remain focused and on track.

Finally, the level of accuracy expected in a thesis or dissertation project is quite high. This will require that you edit your writing to a level that far exceeds what may be expected in a term paper assignment. Not only must your writing conform to the particular style manual used in your field, but it should also be free of mechanical errors. The guidelines in Chapter 9 and the self-editing guide in Chapter 11 will help you accomplish this. Make sure that you allow enough time to set your draft aside for at least a few days prior to editing your writing and expect to use the self-editing guide several times before you give your adviser a draft of the review.

Writing a Literature Review for a Journal Article

The literature review section of a journal article is the most straightforward of the three types of reviews covered in this book. Literature reviews in journal articles are shorter and more focused because their major purpose is to provide the background and rationale for specific and often very narrow research projects.

On the other hand, these reviews will undergo a level of scrutiny that may exceed even that which your thesis or dissertation review underwent. Article submissions for refereed journals are routinely evaluated by two or three of the leading scholars in your area of research. This means that your article should not only reflect the current state of research in your topic, but it should also be error free. Here again, the self-editing checklist from Chapter 11 should be carefully applied.

Frequently, an author will write a journal article a year or more after the research was conducted. This often happens when students decide to write article-length versions of their thesis or dissertation research. If this applies to you, search through the latest issues of the journals in your field to make sure that your literature review cites the very latest work published on your topic.

Although there is some variation among journals, the literature review in a journal article is usually expected to be combined with the introduction, that is, the introduction to the research is an essay that introduces readers to both the topic and purpose of the research while providing an overview of the relevant literature. Therefore, the emphasis of the review should be on establishing the scientific context in which a particular study was conducted and how it contributes to the field. In other words, it should help demonstrate the rationale for the original research reported in the article. As such, it is typically much more narrow and focused than a literature review chapter for a thesis or dissertation.

Activities for Chapter 2

1. What is your purpose for writing a literature review?
   A. As a term paper for a class.
   B. As a chapter for a thesis or dissertation.
   C. As part of the introduction to a journal article.
   D. Other: _____

2. If you are writing a literature review as a term paper, has your instructor assigned you a specific topic to review? If yes, write the topic here. Also write any questions you need to ask your instructor.

3. If you are writing a literature review as a term paper and your instructor has not assigned you a specific topic, briefly describe two or three possible topics here. (If you are at a loss, examine your textbook for ideas.)

4. If you are writing a literature review for a thesis or dissertation, write the topic here.

5. If you are writing a literature review for a thesis or dissertation, what is your timeline for completing the first draft? Share your timeline with your instructor for feedback.

6. If you are writing a literature review for a thesis or dissertation, read the literature review chapters in at least three of the theses or dissertations approved by your committee chair. These are normally housed in the university library. Then, interview your committee chair to clarify the expectations. Make notes here on what you learned about what is expected in such a chapter.

7. If you are writing a literature review for a journal article, name your research purpose or hypothesis. After you have read the literature on your topic, revise your purpose or hypothesis, if necessary, in light of the literature. (Remember that a research purpose or hypothesis should flow directly and logically from the literature reviewed.)

Chapter 3

Selecting a Topic and Identifying Literature for Review

"Where should I begin?" This may be the most commonly asked question by students preparing to write a literature review. While there is no easy answer, this chapter was designed to illustrate the process for getting started used by many professional writers and researchers. Keep in mind that writing is an individual process, so the procedures described here are intended to be used as a road map rather than as a prescription. By working through this chapter, you will be able to develop two important products that will help you begin writing an effective literature review—a written description of your topic and a working draft of your reading list.

Obviously, the first step in any kind of academic writing is to decide what you will write about, but the specific path you follow in working through this step will vary depending on your purpose for writing a literature review. The previous chapter described the three most common reasons for writing literature reviews.

In any of these types of literature reviews, you usually should narrowly define your topic. Example 3.0 presents a topic that is much too general. In fact, it is the title of a survey course taught at many major universities and represents an extensive body of literature.

Example 3.0

General Topic: Child Language Acquisition

Obviously, the topic in Example 3.0 will have to be narrowed down considerably before it can be used effectively to produce a manageable literature review. The steps that follow will guide you through a process that will result in better alternatives to this example.

✓ Step 1: Search an appropriate database.

Before you select a database and search it, you need to select at least a general topic. Let's suppose you select this topic: Child Language Acquisition, which is general and will yield more references than you can possibly use, as you will see below. Nevertheless, it is usually all right to start with a general topic, see how much literature there is on it, and then narrow the topic to a more manageable one, a process that you will learn about in this chapter.

A general search using the topic in Example 3.0 will yield many thousands of records. Therefore, you should specify a set of parameters that will give you a focused result. For example, you can limit your search to journal articles, which is recommended; or you can specify a limited range of publication dates, perhaps going back three to five years, which is also recommended. A sample search conducted in the Educational Resource Information Center (ERIC) database using the general topic in Example 3.0 yielded the results in Example 3.1.1, presented in the order of the steps followed.

Example 3.1.1

Step	Number of Records
Search with descriptor "language acquisition":	13,826
Limit search to journal articles AND to publication dates of 1995-present:	787
Further limit the search to "child language":	107

Note that for each article that is identified by the database, you will be given an abstract and a list of *descriptors*. These are the terms and phrases that describe the article's contents. Most databases compile descriptors in a *thesaurus*,[1] which is a kind of glossary or wordbook containing the major subject-matter terms used in a given field of study. For example, the descriptors "child language" and "language acquisition" are among thousands of descriptors found in the ERIC thesaurus. In the search of a database, the connectors "AND" and "OR" will produce vastly different results. For example, "language acquisition" AND "child language" will produce fewer references than "language acquisition" OR "child language" because the former selects entries that have both descriptors present whereas the latter selects entries that contain at least one of the two descriptors. See Appendix A for a brief explanation of how to use such connectors when searching electronic databases.

Appendix B contains the 107 records obtained by using the procedures described here. Note that the ERIC database was used in this example because its holdings are comprehensive and encompass several disciplines with an emphasis on education. Other databases, such as PsycINFO, which is oriented toward psychology, would produce results that focus on other disciplines. More specific recommendations for conducting a search using your library's on-line databases are discussed in the next section. For now, let us assume that Appendix B represents our first look at the available literature for this topic.[2]

---

[1] If the database you are using has a thesaurus, you can either review it on-line or you can consult a printed version in the reference section of your library.

[2] You should note that the records in Appendix B are reproduced here exactly as they were given by ERIC, and that this is not an acceptable format for a finished reference list or bibliography. Consult the appropriate style manual in your subject area for guidance in recasting it in an acceptable form.

✔ Step 2: Shorten your list to a manageable size.

Although Appendix B is comprehensive, it is too broad for use in a typical literature review. It includes articles written by developmental psychologists, theoretical linguists, second-language researchers, anthropologists, and educators, among others. It is unlikely that a single course in Child Language Acquisition will encompass all these areas. Therefore, you should *determine which of these articles pertain to your major field of study* and eliminate those that do not. If the remaining list still appears too broad, *consider reclassifying the amended list*. For example, a linguistics major will find that roughly one-third of the entries in Appendix B deal with children's acquisition of specific language features. On further examination, you can distinguish between articles that deal with grammatical categories—such as verbs, plurals, and sentences—and articles that deal with the sound system—such as vowels, consonants, and stress—either of which will reduce your list considerably. Third, if the title of an article is difficult to classify, *consider whether the journal in which it appeared is of interest to researchers in your field*. You can often determine this by simply considering the title of the journal. For example, the journal titled *Studies in Second Language Acquisition* (see reference number 74 in Appendix B) probably carries articles of interest to a different group of professionals than the journal titled *Journal of Speech and Hearing Research* (see reference number 97). Likewise, examining the titles of the articles will give you a strong indication of the fields with which the references are most closely allied.

Example 3.2.1 presents seven possible revised topics based on the sample ERIC search. In this example, the revised topics illustrate the reclassification of Appendix B according to major areas of study that can be discerned from a review of the titles of the articles. Note that these major areas correspond to some of the academic departments which may offer courses in child language acquisition—linguistics, psychology, education, child development, and language disorders. Depending on the specific nature of your course and on the academic department in which it is offered, you can now narrow your topic area by selecting one of the topics in Example 3.2.1. These classifications are given merely to illustrate the process. In fact, Appendix B can be reclassified into numerous other categories.

Example 3.2.1
Possible Topic Areas, with Reference Numbers from Appendix B, Sample ERIC Search:

Role of Parents in Child Language Acquisition
> *Sample reference numbers*: 23, 30, 34, 42, 64, 69, 70, 83, 84, 88, 89, 100

Language Acquisition in Deaf Children
> *Sample reference numbers*: 6, 30, 42, 46, 50, 51, 88, 106

Children's Acquisition of Grammatical Categories
> *Sample reference numbers*: 6, 11, 12, 13, 14, 15, 16, 17, 19, 24, 26, 27, 28, 33, 35, 37, 38, 39, 41, 43, 44, 45, 48, 55, 56, 58, 65, 69, 72, 74, 76, 78, 81, 90, 95, 96, 98, 102, 103, 105

Children's Acquisition of the Sound System
> *Sample reference numbers*: 2, 6, 10, 21, 25, 36, 46, 66, 67, 68, 73, 97

Children's Acquisition of Lexical Items (Words)
> *Sample reference numbers*: 1, 3, 5, 19, 20, 31, 38, 53, 56, 62, 63, 64, 80, 82, 83, 84, 86, 94, 97, 104

Relation between Children's Cognitive and Language Development
> *Sample reference numbers*: 8, 9, 32, 40, 47, 61, 77

Second Language Acquisition
> *Sample reference numbers*: 13, 18, 22, 29, 49, 54, 57, 59, 60, 70, 71, 72, 74, 75, 82, 83, 94, 99

✔ Step 3: Write the first draft of your topic statement.

Now that you have narrowed your search results, you can reexamine the more focused list of articles you have generated and choose a more specific topic for your literature review. It is premature for you to decide on a final topic. This can come only after you have read some of the articles you have located. However, the first draft of your topic statement should attempt to name the area you will investigate. Think of this statement as a descriptive phrase rather than as a paper or chapter title. Example 3.3.1 presents two topic statements, one for a literature review in the area of linguistics, and the other in psychology. Note that these first drafts are still very general. The remaining steps in this chapter will help you narrow down your topic statement.

Example 3.3.1

Linguistics:
Children's acquisition of features of language

Psychology:
The development of language and thought in children

✔ Step 4: Familiarize yourself with on-line databases.

All university libraries now subscribe to on-line electronic databases. The manual searches of the past have given way to computerized searches. Therefore, it is essential that you familiarize yourself with your campus library's computer resources. If you are new to on-line databases, you should attend a workshop or class to learn how to use these services, and pick up and carefully read all the handouts concerning your university's database resources. As noted earlier, this book will show you only how to approach databases in general—not the specific features of any of them.

✓ Step 5: Identify the relevant databases in your field of study.

Every academic field has developed its own database services that are used by its students and scholars. Early in your search, you should identify the databases specific to your field of study. In addition to the information you receive in the library, you should ask your adviser or instructor about the preferred databases in your major. You can then find out where they are available and whether they can be accessed from your home or dormitory.

Table 1 illustrates the range of database resources available through the California State University, Los Angeles (CSU, Los Angeles) library, as an example. This list is by no means exhaustive; in fact, larger research libraries will have many more research services than are listed in this table. If you are a student at a small university, it is recommended that you investigate whether your university's library maintains cooperative arrangements with larger institutions in your area.

Table 1   Summary of Selected Library Databases

Database	Subject Areas	Database Statistics
Basic Biosis	Life Science	300,000 records from 350 journals 1994-present, updated monthly
CINAHL	Nursing, Allied Health, Biomedical and Consumer Health	352,000 records from 900 journals 1982-present, updated quarterly
Dissertation Abstracts	Complete range of academic subjects	1,566,000 records 1861-present, updated monthly
ERIC	Education and related fields	956,000 records from journals, books, theses, and unpublished reports 1966-present, updated monthly
LLBA	Linguistics and Language Behavior Abstracts	250,000 records from journals, books, dissertations, book reviews, and other media 1973-present, updated quarterly
Medline	Nursing, Public Health, Pharmacy, Sports Medicine, Psychiatry, Dentistry, and Veterinary Medicine	9,305,000 records, including articles from 3,500 journals published internationally 1985-present, updated monthly
MLA	Literature, Language, Linguistics, and Folklore	1,308,000 records from 4,000 US and international journals 1963-present, updated monthly

Continued on next page.

Table 1 Continued

NCJRS	Corrections, Drugs & Crime, Juvenile Justice, Law Enforcement, Statistics, and Victims	140,000 records, including journal articles, government documents, and unpublished reports 1970-present, updated periodically
PAIS International	Social Sciences, emphasis on contemporary social, economic, and political issues, and on public policy	451,000 records from journals 1972-present, updated monthly
PsycINFO	Psychology and related fields	1,249,000 records from 1,300 journals 1887-present, updated monthly
Social Sciences Abstracts	Sociology, Psychology, Anthropology, Geography, Economics, Political Science, and Law	562,000 records from 400 journals 1983-present, updated monthly
Social Work Abstracts	Social Work and related fields	30,000 records from journals 1977-present, updated quarterly
Sociological Abstracts	Sociology, Social Work, and other social sciences	519,000 records from 3,000 journals 1963-present, updated bimonthly
Sport Discus	Sports Medicine, Physical Education, Exercise, Physiology, Biomechanics, Psychology, Training, Coaching, and Nutrition	344,000 records 1970-present, updated quarterly

✔ Step 6: Familiarize yourself with the organization of the database.

The on-line databases described in Table 1 contain abstracts of several kinds of documents, including journal articles, books, conference presentations, project reports, and government documents. As you know from Chapter 1, this book focuses on reviewing articles in academic journals. For each of the thousands of journal articles in these databases, there is a single *record* with specific information about the article. In other words, each item on the list of titles you derive from your search of a database will be linked to an expanded description organized according to a set of categories of information. For instance, each of these records contains a number of *fields*, which include the article's title, author, source journal, publication date, abstract, and list of descriptors (terms and phrases that describe the article's contents). You can narrow the scope of a search by manipulating one or more of these fields. Publication date, source journal, and author are often used to narrow a search, but the most common method of searching a database is by specifying one or more descriptors. This method is covered next.

✓ Step 7: Begin with a general descriptor; then limit the output.

Unless you have had previous knowledge of a particular topic, you should begin a search with a general descriptor from the database's thesaurus. If a thesaurus is not available, use a label or phrase that describes the topic you are investigating. If this procedure results in too many references, you can then limit the search by adding additional descriptors using *and*. For example, if you search for "social" *and* "phobia," you will get only articles that mention *both* of these terms. Here is an example: Searching the major database in psychology, PsycINFO, from 1995 to present yields 770 documents (mainly journal articles) relating to "phobia." A search for "social" *and* "phobia" for the same time period yields 441 documents. Finally, a search for "children," *and* "social," *and* "phobia" yields only 40 documents.

Another effective technique for limiting the number of documents retrieved from an electronic database is to limit the search to descriptors that appear in only the title and/or abstract (summary of the article), restrictions that are permitted in PsycINFO and some other databases. Using these restrictions will help to eliminate articles in which the descriptor is mentioned only in passing in the body of the article since an article dealing primarily with phobias would almost certainly mention the term in one of these important places. (Note that in an unrestricted search, the contents of entire documents are searched.) A search of PsycINFO restricting the search for "phobia" in only the titles and abstracts from 1995 to the present yields a total of 322 documents, which is substantially less than the 770 retrieved in an unrestricted search. With the restriction that "phobia" appear in *both* the title and abstract, 294 articles were obtained.

✓ Step 8: Use "on topic" records to refine the search.

As pointed out, the database's thesaurus is a good source of the key subject-matter terms used in that discipline, but another good source of more specific descriptors is a record from a previous search you conducted on a topic. In other words, once you find a record that deals specifically with your area of interest, you should review that record's descriptors for clues on how to further refine your search.

✓ Step 9: Redefine your topic more narrowly.

Selecting a reasonably narrow topic is essential if you are to defend your selection of a topic and write an effective review on it. Topics that are too broad will stretch your limits of energy and time—especially if you are writing a review for a term project in a class that lasts only one semester. A review of a topic that is too broad very likely will lead to a review that is superficial, jumps from area to area within the topic, and fails to demonstrate to your reader that you have thoroughly mastered the literature on the topic. Thus, at this point, you should consider redefining your topic more narrowly.

Example 3.9.1 presents a topic that is problematic for at least two reasons. First, it is much too broadly defined. Even though the writer has limited the review to English-speaking children as old as four years, it would be difficult to eliminate very many entries from Appendix B, leaving the writer with many more references than are needed. Second, this topic lacks a specific focus. Apparently, the writer has chosen to consider studies of children acquiring both the sound and the grammatical systems. If so, the finished review will either be a book-length manuscript (or two) or a superficial treatment of the literature.

Example 3.9.1
A topic that is too broad for most purposes:

This paper deals with child language acquisition. I will review the literature that deals with how children learn to speak in a naturalistic setting, starting with the earliest sounds and progressing to fully formed sentences. I will limit myself to English-speaking children, aged zero to four years.

Example 3.9.2 is an improved version of the topic. Note that this writer has narrowed the focus of the review to a specific part of language. The writer has stated clearly that the review has two main goals—to catalog the range of verbal features that have been studied and to describe what is known about the route children follow in acquiring them. Even though it is very likely that this topic will be modified several more times, based on the careful reading of the studies found, it is sufficiently focused to provide the writer with a reasonable first cut of the studies in Appendix B.

Example 3.9.2
An improved topic description:

This paper describes what is known about how children acquire the ability to describe time and to make references to time, including the use of verbs and other features contained in the verb phrase. I will attempt, first, to describe the range of verb phrase features that have been studied, and second, to describe the path children follow as they develop greater linguistic competence with reference to time.

✓ Step 10: Start with the most current, and work backwards.

The most effective way to begin a search in a field that is new to you is to start with the most current articles. If you judge a current article to be relevant to your topic, the article's reference list or bibliography will provide useful clues about how to pursue your review of the literature. In Appendix B, for example, a good strategy would be to review articles from the first two or three pages (all of which are recent because the search was restricted to documents from 1995 to the present)[3], photocopy the reference lists from the actual articles in the library, compare those lists against the contents of Appendix B, and make strategic decisions about rounding out your reading list. Keep in mind two important criteria for developing your reading list: (a) the reading list should represent the extent of knowledge about the topic and (b) it should provide a proper context for your own investigation.

✓ Step 11: Search for theoretical articles on your topic.

As you learned in Chapter 1, theoretical articles that relate directly to your topic should be included in your literature review. However, a typical search of the literature in the social and behavioral sciences will yield primarily original reports of empirical research because these types of documents dominate academic journals. If you have difficulty locating theoretical articles on your topic, include "theory" as one of your descriptors. A search of the PsycINFO database using the descriptors "social" *and* "phobia" *and* "theory" yielded 11 documents, including the one in Example 3.11.1, which would clearly be useful for someone planning to write in this area.

> **Example 3.11.1**
> *An article obtained by using the term "theory" in the search:*
>
> Herbert, J. D. (1995). An overview of the current status of social phobia. *Applied and Preventive Psychology*, *4*, 39–51. [The abstract begins: Reviews the literature on social phobia and provides a general accounting of the disorder. Social phobia is defined and *theories* (emphasis added) about its etiology are presented, including....]

Notice that this article also presents a review of literature, which relates to the next step.

It is also important to keep in mind that writers of empirical research reports will often discuss the relationship of various theories to their work and provide references to the theoretical literature. You should follow up these leads by looking up the references.

✓ Step 12: Look for "review" articles.

A corollary to the search technique described in the previous step is to use the descriptor "review" as a means of locating review articles. Previously published review articles are very useful in planning a new literature review

---

[3] Note that the sample literature search in Appendix B was restricted to a three-year period primarily for space constraints. As a rule, you are advised to restrict your search to a five-year period to establish currency.

because they are helpful in identifying the breadth and scope of the literature in a field of study. They usually will include a much more comprehensive reference list than is typical in a research article.

Note that some journals only publish literature reviews, some emphasize original reports of empirical research but occasionally will publish literature review articles by leading researchers in a field who seek to describe the "state of the art" in a particular topic, and others have editorial policies against publishing reviews. If you know the names of journals in your field that publish reviews, you might specify their names in a database search.[4] Because this will restrict your search to just those journals, this should be a separate search from your main one.

A search of PsycINFO using "substance abuse," and "treatment," and "review" as descriptors identified two potentially useful review articles on the treatment of substance abusers. These are shown in Example 3.12.1.

Example 3.12.1

Two articles obtained by using "review" in the search:

Crits-Christoph, P., & Siqueland, J. (1996). Psychosocial treatment for drug abuse: Selected review and recommendations for national health care. *Archives of General Psychiatry, 53,* 749–756. [The abstract begins: Reviews of selected research articles relevant to the psychosocial treatment of substance abuse (excluding alcohol abuse)....]

Weinber, N. Z. et al. (1998). Adolescent substance abuse: A review of the past 10 years. *Journal of the American Academy of Child and Adolescent Psychiatry, 37,* 252–261. [The abstract begins: Reviews and synthesizes the scientific literature on adolescent substance abuse since publication of G. W. Bailey's (1989) review on substance abuse in youth. The present review covers natural history,...treatment, and prevention....]

Notice that the Weinber et al. (1998) review article leads to an earlier review by Bailey (1989), which would certainly be of interest.

✓ Step 13: Identify the landmark or classic studies.

Finally, it is important to identify the landmark studies on your topic. Unfortunately, some students believe that this is an optional nicety. However, without at least a passing knowledge of landmark studies, you will not understand the present context for your chosen topic. If you are writing a thesis or dissertation, in which fairly exhaustive reviews are expected, a failure to reference the landmark studies might be regarded as a serious, if not fatal, flaw.

---

[4] In psychology, for example, *Psychological Bulletin* is an important journal devoted to literature reviews. A premier review journal in education is *Review of Educational Research.*

It is not always easy to identify landmark studies at the very beginning of a literature search. Some review articles will note the landmark studies explicitly, and occasionally the author of an original report of empirical research will point them out as was done in Example 3.13.1.

Example 3.13.1[5]
Excerpt from a research article that identifies a landmark study:

For example, in a study which has now become a *classic* (emphasis added), Weitz (1972) administered a questionnaire assessing White-Black racial attitudes to a university population. For many of her subjects...(p. 2172)

While reading the articles you selected, you often will notice that certain authors' names are mentioned over and over. For example, if you read extensively on how social factors affect learning, you will probably find that Albert Bandura's social learning theory is cited by numerous authors of research articles. At this point, you would want to search the database again using Bandura's first and last name as one of the descriptors for two reasons: (1) to locate material he has written on his theory (keep in mind that you want it from the *original source* and not just someone else's paraphrase) and (2) to try to locate any early studies that he may have conducted that led him to the theory or that he originally presented to lend credence to the theory. Keep in mind that people who present theories very often conduct research and publish it in support of their theories. Their early studies that helped establish their theories are the ones that are most likely to be considered "landmark" or "classic." Note that when you conduct such a search of the database, you should *not* restrict the search to only articles published in recent years. Searching all years of the PsycINFO database restricting the search to articles with the name "Albert Bandura" as the author of the article, *and* "social" in the title of the article, and "learning" in all fields, yields relevant documents, including this early one:

Example 3.13.2
An early study by a leading researcher and theoritician:

Bandura, A. (1969). Social learning of moral judgments. *Journal of Personality and Social Psychology, 11*, 275–279.

Finally, consult the textbook for your course. Textbook authors often briefly trace the history of thought on important topics and may well mention what they believe to be the classic studies.

---

[5] Page, S. (1997). An unobtrusive measure of racial behavior in a university cafeteria. *The Journal of Applied Social Psychology, 27*, 2172-2176.

Activities for Chapter 3

1. First, become familiar with the electronic databases in your field (ERIC, PsycINFO, etc.). You can do so either by attending a workshop in your university library or by reading the documentation and practicing on your own. Note that many libraries now allow you to search their databases on-line from your home, but you will probably need to use a university computer account to do so. Once you are familiar with the databases, select one to complete the following steps.

2. If your instructor has assigned a term paper on a specific topic, search the database using a simple phrase that describes this topic. If you are working on your own, select an area that interests you, and search the database using a simple phrase that describes your area of interest.
 - How many sources did the search produce?

3. Retrieve two or three records from your search, and locate the lists of descriptors. Compare the three lists and note the areas of commonality as well as difference.
 - Write down the exact wording of three descriptors that relate to your intended topic. You should choose descriptors that reflect your own personal interest in the topic.
 - Compared to the simple phrase you used when you started, do you think these descriptors are more specific or more general? Why?

4. Now, use the descriptors you just located to modify the search.
 - First, modify the search to select more records.
 - Then, modify the search to select fewer records.
 - If you used the connector AND, did it result in more or fewer sources? Why do you think this happened?
 - If you used the connector OR, did it result in more or fewer sources? Why do you think this happened?

5. If necessary, narrow the search further until you have between 100-200 sources, and print out the search results.
 - Carefully scan the printed list to identify several possible subcategories.
 - Compare the new categories to your original topic.
 - Redefine your topic more narrowly, and identify the articles that pertain to your new topic. Prepare a typed list of these articles.

Chapter 4

General Guidelines for Analyzing Literature

Now that you have identified the preliminary set of articles for your review, you should begin the process of analyzing them *prior to* beginning to write your review. This chapter is designed to help you through this process. The end result will be two important products—a working draft of your reference list and the set of note cards that will contain specific, detailed information about each article, both of which you will need before you begin to write.

✔ Guideline 1: Scan the articles to get an overview of each one.

Obviously, you read the titles of the articles when you selected them, and you probably also read the abstracts (i.e., summaries) that most journals include near the beginning of each article. Next you should read the first few paragraphs of each article, where the author usually provides a general introduction to his or her problem area. This will give you a feel for the author's writing style as well as his or her general perspectives on the research problem. Then jump to the last paragraph before the heading "Method," which is usually the first major heading in the text of a research article. This is the traditional paragraph in which researchers explicitly state their specific hypotheses, research questions, or research purposes. Next, scan the rest of the article, noting all headings and subheadings. Scan the text in each subsection, but do not allow yourself to get caught up in the details or any points that seem difficult or confusing. Your purpose at this point is to get only an overview.

Example 4.1.1 shows in bold a typical set of major headings for a short report of original research in a journal article.

Example 4.1.1

Title [followed by authors' names and their institutional affiliations]
Abstract [a summary of the complete report]
[An introduction in which related literature is reviewed follows the abstract; typically, there is *no* heading called "Introduction."]
Method
    Participants [or Subjects]
    Measures [or Measurement, Observation, or Instrumentation]
Results
Discussion [or Discussion and Conclusions and Implications]

Longer articles will often contain additional headings such as *assumptions*, *definitions, experimental treatments, limitations*, and so on. Scanning each of these sections will help prepare you to navigate when you begin to read the article in detail from beginning to end.

The last heading in a research article is usually called "Discussion" or "Discussion and Conclusions." Researchers often reiterate their major findings in the first few paragraphs under this heading. Reading them will help you when you read the results section in detail, which can be difficult if it contains numerous statistics.

Note that by following this guideline you will be *pre-reading*—a technique widely recommended by specialists in reading as the first step in reading a technical report. Because pre-reading gives you an overview of the purpose and contents of a report, it helps you keep your eye on the big picture as you subsequently work though a research report from beginning to end. The information you gain by pre-reading will also help you group the articles into categories, as suggested in the next guideline.

✓ Guideline 2: Based on your overview (see Guideline 1), group the articles by categories.

Sort the articles you have amassed into stacks that correspond roughly to the categories of studies you will describe. You may choose to organize them in any number of ways, but the most common practice is to organize them, first, by topics and subtopics, and then in chronological order within each subtopic. Example 4.2.1 shows a possible grouping of articles for a review of research literature on *affirmative action in higher education* into categories and subcategories:

Example 4.2.1[1]

I. Background Issues
      A. General Historical Background
      B. History of Affirmative Action in Higher Education
      C. Philosophical Basis
      D. The Law and Affirmative Action
II. The Effects of Affirmative Action
      A. Effects on Minority Enrollment
      B. Effects on Academic Achievement
      C. Other Effects
III. Criticisms of Affirmative Action
IV. Alternatives to Affirmative Action

---

[1] This outline is patterned on Tierney, W. G. (1997). The parameters of affirmative action: Equity and excellence in the academy. *Review of Educational Research, 67,* 165–196.

Organizing the articles into categories will facilitate your analysis if you read all the articles in each category/subcategory at about the same time. For instance, it will be easier to synthesize the literature on the effects of affirmative action on minority enrollment in higher education if all the articles on this topic are read together, starting with the most recent one.

✔ Guideline 3: Organize yourself before reading the articles.

It is important to organize yourself prior to beginning a detailed reading of the articles. You will need a computer, a pack of note cards to write your comments on, and several packs of self-adhesive flags that you can use to identify noteworthy comments. You can use different colored self-stick flags to mark different subtopics, different research methods, a review article or landmark study, or anything else that should be noted or might help you organize your review. If you are using a computer, you can use different colors of highlighting (available on modern word processing programs) instead of colored flags on note cards.

✔ Guideline 4: Use a consistent format in your notes.

Once you have organized the articles, you should begin to read them. As you read, summarize the important points and write them on the note cards.

Develop a format for recording your notes about the articles you will be reading, and use this same format consistently. Building consistency into your notes at this stage in the process will pay off later when you start to write the review. As has been noted, you will encounter considerable variation across studies, and your notes should be consistent and detailed enough for you to be able to describe both differences and similarities across them. Example 4.4.1 illustrates the recommended format for recording your notes. Remember to note the page numbers whenever you copy an author's words verbatim; direct quotations should always be accompanied by page numbers, and it will save you considerable time later in the process if you already have the page numbers noted. Make sure to double-check your quotes for accuracy.

Example 4.4.1
Author(s)' Last name(s), Initial(s).
Title of Article
Publication Year
Name of Journal/Volume/Number/Page Numbers
_____
Notes (*responding to the following questions*)
1. What is the main point of this article?
2. Describe the methodology used. (Include numbers of subjects, controls, treatments, etc.)
3. Describe the findings.

4. What, if anything, is notable about this article? (Is it a landmark study? Does it have flaws? Is it an experimental study? Is it qualitative or quantitative?, and so on.)
5. Note specific details you find relevant. (Make this as long as necessary.)

The points in Example 4.4.1 are given as examples to guide you through this process. In an actual case, you may choose to disregard one or more of them or you may decide that others are more appropriate. Obviously, you will need to create several note cards per source. For example, you might have a card for each article on the main point of the article, another one on the research methodology used, and so on.

It may also be helpful to use a separate card on which you make note of questions or concerns you have as you read a particular article, or on which you note any conclusions you may reach about the subject of the research. These notes can later be incorporated into your paper, perhaps in your discussion or conclusion, and using a separate card for this will save you valuable time later.

Use paper clips or rubber bands to keep your cards on a given article together; this will help you avoid repeating the bibliographical details on every card.

✓ Guideline 5: Look for explicit definitions of key terms in the literature.

It should not surprise you that different researchers sometimes define key terms in different ways. If there are major differences of opinion on how the variables you will be writing about should be defined, you will want to make notes on the definitions. In fact, if a number of different definitions are offered, you might find it helpful to prepare a separate set of cards containing just the definitions.

To see the importance of how terms are defined, consider definitions of the variable called *family secrets*. The definition in Example 4.5.1 clearly has a negative overtone. The one in Example 4.5.2 is more neutral, allowing for inclusion of a secret that is not negatively viewed by society—such as a surprise birthday party that is kept a secret from one of the family members.

Example 4.5.1[2]

Warren and Laslett (1977) view family secrets as concealing something negatively valued: a strategy used to not only hide acts that are morally ill reputed but also to avoid the stigma associated with them.

---

[2] Brown-Smith, N. (1988). Family secrets. *Journal of Family Issues, 19*, p. 22.

Example 4.5.2[3]

…a family secret is any information that directly affects or concerns one but is either withheld or differentially shared between or among family members.

Clearly, different researchers may come to different conclusions about the nature and effects of family secrets simply because their definitions differ in important respects. Noting such differences will help you better understand the literature you are analyzing and prepare you to define key terms in your literature review.

✔ Guideline 6: Look for methodological strengths.

It is unlikely that you will find a single article with the definitive statement about any aspect of the human condition. Inevitably, some studies will be stronger than others, and these strengths should be noted in your review. Ask yourself how strong the evidence is, and keep in mind that in your role as the reviewer you have the right and the responsibility to make these subjective evaluations.

The strength of an article may come from the methodology used. Do the research methods of one study improve on the data-gathering techniques of earlier studies? Does the article's strength derive from the size and generalizability of its subject pool? Does a set of studies demonstrate that the same conclusion can be reached by using a variety of methods? These and other similar questions will guide you in determining the strengths of particular studies.

As noted in Chapter 1, it is assumed that all students who take the time to read the literature carefully can make broad general assessments of the major strengths and weaknesses (see the next guideline) of empirical studies. For more advanced students, additional guidelines are presented in Chapter 5.

✔ Guideline 7: Look for methodological weaknesses.

Remember that you should note any major weaknesses you encounter when reviewing research literature. The same process you used in identifying strengths should be used when identifying weaknesses. For example, you should determine whether the author's research method has provided new insights into the research topic. Particularly if an innovative methodology is used, does it seem appropriate, or does it raise the possibility of alternative explanations? Has an appropriate sample been used? Are the findings consistent with those of similar studies? Is enough evidence presented in the article for a reasonable person to judge whether the researcher's conclusions are valid?

Here again, it may be preferable to critique groups of studies together, especially if their flaws are similar. Generally, it is *inappropriate* to note each and

---

[3] Brown-Smith, N. (1988). Family secrets. *Journal of Family Issues, 19*, p. 24.

every flaw in every study you review. Instead, note major weaknesses of individual studies, and keep your eye out for patterns of weaknesses across groups of studies. For example, if all the research reports on a subtopic you are reviewing are based on very small samples, you might note this fact on a separate card that relates to the collection of articles on that subtopic. Once you have reached your conclusions, you may want to check your impressions by asking your instructor for feedback.

✓ Guideline 8: Distinguish between assertion and evidence.

A very common mistake made in literature reviews is to report an author's assertions as though they were findings. To avoid this mistake, make sure you have understood the author's evidence and its interpretation. A finding derives from the evidence presented; an assertion is the author's opinion. Suppose a number of authors had made a common assertion about conflict resolution programs, and you reported it in your literature review as shown in Example 4.8.1. Making this statement in the context of a review of research literature may mislead your readers into believing these are conclusions based on research data when they are actually assertions.

Example 4.8.1

Conflict-resolution programs are being implemented in many schools because they reduce suspensions and detentions, referrals to the principal, and absenteeism, while increasing students' self-confidence, time spent on academic tasks, and academic achievement (Araki, 1990; David, 1986; Lam, 1989; Marshall, 1987; Maxwell, 1989; Tolson, McDonald, & Moriarty, 1992).

In Example 4.8.2, the reviewer clearly indicates that they are assertions. You will be able to make such distinctions when you write your literature review only if you make the distinction between evidence and assertion in your notes while analyzing literature.

Example 4.8.2[4]

Although conflict-resolution programs are being implemented in many schools, there has been little empirical research on their effectiveness. Advocates for conflict-resolution programs in schools *have asserted* (emphasis added) that the programs reduce suspensions and detentions, referrals to the principal, and absenteeism, while increasing students' self-

---

[4] Stevahn, L., Johnson, D.W., Johnson, R.T., Green, K., & Laginski, A. M. (1997). Effects on high school students of conflict-resolution training integrated into English literature. *The Journal of Social Psychology, 137*, 302-315.

confidence, time spent on academic tasks, and academic achievement (Araki, 1990; Davis, 1986; Lam, 1989; Marshall, 1987; Maxwell, 1989; Tolson, McDonald, & Moriarty, 1992). (p. 303)

This same caution should be exercised in your own writing as well. That is, you should avoid making assertions that are not substantiated by the research you have reviewed unless you clearly label them as your assertions.

✓ Guideline 9: Identify the major trends or patterns in the results of previous studies.

When you write your literature review, you will be responsible for pointing out major trends or patterns in the results reported in the research articles you review. This may take the form of a *generalization*, in which you generalize from the various articles, such as is done in Example 4.9.1. Note that the references that support the generalization in the example were cited earlier in the review in which this excerpt appeared.

Example 4.9.1[5]

The review suggests strongly that those who wish to increase parental involvement and extend the benefits it offers must focus at least in part on the parent's perspective on the process. Parents who believe they should be involved in their children's education and schooling *and* who have a positive sense of efficacy about the usefulness of their involvement are likely to be involved.

Of course, you may not be as fortunate as the reviewer who wrote Example 4.9.1. There may be considerable inconsistencies from article to article. When this happens, you should try to make sense of them for your reader. For example, you might state a generalization based on a *majority* of the articles, or you might state a generalization based only on those articles you think have the strongest research methodology. Either option is acceptable as long as you clearly describe to your reader the basis for your generalization. Once again, careful note taking during the analysis stage will help you in this process.

✓ Guideline 10: Identify gaps in the literature.

It is every graduate student's dream to discover a significant gap in the literature, especially one that can form the crux of the student's thesis or dissertation study. In fact, gaps often exist because research in these areas present considerable obstacles for researchers. These gaps should be noted in a literature

---

[5] Hoover-Dempsey, K. V., Sandler, H. M. (1997). Why do parents become involved in their children's education? *Review of Educational Research, 67,* 3–42 (p. 36).

review, along with discussions of why they exist. If you identify a gap that you believe should be addressed, make note of it, and take it into consideration as you plan the organization of your review, which is the subject of the following chapter.

✓ Guideline 11: Identify relationships among studies.

As you read additional articles on your list, make note of any relationships that may exist among studies. For example, a landmark article may have spawned a new approach subsequently explored in additional studies conducted by others, or two articles may explore the same or similar question but with different age groups or language groups. It is important to point out these relationships in your review. When you write, you probably will want to discuss related ones together.

✓ Guideline 12: Note how each reviewed article relates to your topic.

Try to keep your review focused on the topic you have chosen. It is inappropriate to include studies that bear no relationship to your area of study in your literature review. Therefore, your notes should include explicit references to the specific aspects of a study that relate to your topic.

If you determine that there is no literature with a direct bearing on one or more aspects of your research topic, it is permissible to review peripheral research, but this should be done cautiously. Pyrczak and Bruce (1998)[6] cite the example of year-round school schedules, which were implemented in Los Angeles as a curricular innovation.

Example 4.12.1

When Los Angeles first started implementing year-round school schedules, for example, there was no published research on the topic. There was research, however, on traditional school-year programs in which children attended school in shifts, on the effects of the length of the school year on achievement, and on the effectiveness of summer school programs. Students who were writing theses and dissertations on the Los Angeles program had to cite such peripheral literature in order to demonstrate their ability to conduct a search of the literature and write a comprehensive, well-organized review of literature. (p. 43)

Such examples are rare, and you are advised to consult your instructor before you reach the conclusion that no studies have dealt with your specific research topic.

---

[6] Pyrczak, F. & Bruce, R. R. (1998). *Writing empirical research reports: A basic guide for students of the social and behavioral sciences.* Los Angeles: Pyrczak Publishing.

✓ Guideline 13: Evaluate your reference list for currency and for coverage.

When you have finished reading the articles you have collected, you should reevaluate your entire reference list once more to ensure that it is complete and up to date. A literature review should demonstrate that it represents the latest work done in the subject area. As a rule of thumb, use a five-year span from the present as a tentative limit of coverage, keeping in mind that you will extend farther back when it is warranted. If your review is intended to present a historical overview of your topic, for example, you may have to reach well beyond the five-year span. However, remember that the reader of a literature review expects that you have reported the most current research available. Thus, you should make explicit your reasons for including articles that are not current (e.g., Is it a landmark study? Does it present the only evidence available on a given topic? Does it help you to understand the evolution of a research technique?).

The question of how much literature is enough to include in a review is difficult to answer. In general, your first priority should be to establish that you have read the most current research available. Then, you should try to cover your topic as completely as necessary, not as completely as possible. Your instructor or faculty adviser can help you determine how much is enough.

Activities for Chapter 4

Directions: Refer to the printed list of sources you developed in Activity 5 on page 28.

1. Obtain copies of two articles from this list, and scan each of the articles.
    - Do the authors include a summary of the contents of the literature review at or near the beginning? If so, highlight or mark this summary for future reference.
    - Did the authors use subheadings?
    - Scan the paragraph(s) immediately preceding the heading "Method." Did the authors describe their hypotheses, research questions, or research purposes?
    - Without rereading any of the text of the article, write a brief statement describing what each article is about.

2. Based on your overview of all the articles on your list, make predictions of some of the likely categories and subcategories for your review. Reread the printed list of sources and try to group them by these categories and

subcategories. Then, using these categories and subcategories, create an outline for describing the area of your topic.

3. Carefully review your outline and select the articles you will read first. Within each category, start with the earliest study and work toward the present. You now have your initial reading list.

Chapter 5

Analyzing Literature from the Viewpoint of a Researcher

In the previous chapter, you were advised to make notes on important methodological strengths and weaknesses of the research articles you are reading prior to writing your literature review. This chapter will provide you with information on some points you may want to note regarding research methodology. Those of you who have taken a course in research methods will recognize that this chapter contains only a very brief overview of some of the important issues.

✔ Guideline 1: Note whether the research is quantitative or qualitative.

Because quantitative researchers reduce information to statistics such as averages, percentages, and so on, their research articles are easy to spot. If an article has a results section devoted mainly to the presentation of statistical data, it is a safe bet that it is quantitative. The quantitative approach to research has dominated the social and behavioral sciences throughout the 1900s, so for most topics, you are likely to locate many more articles reporting quantitative than qualitative research.

The literature on how to conduct quantitative research *emphasizes*:

1. Starting with one or more explicitly stated hypotheses that will remain unchanged throughout the study.[1] The hypotheses are reevaluated only after the data have been analyzed.
2. Selecting a random sample (like drawing names out of a hat) from a particular population, if possible.
3. Using a relatively large sample of participants, sometimes as many as 1,500 for a national survey.[2]
4. Measuring with instruments that can be scored objectively such as multiple-choice achievement tests and forced-choice questionnaires in response to which participants mark choices on a scale ranging from strongly agree to strongly disagree.

---

[1] Quantitative researchers sometimes start with specific research questions or purposes instead of a hypothesis.

[2] Even larger samples are sometimes used when large numbers of participants are readily available. Much smaller samples are sometimes used by quantitative researchers, especially when they lack the resources to study larger samples.

5. Presenting results using statistics and making inferences to the population from which the sample was drawn (i.e., inferring that what they found by studying a sample is similar to what they would have found if they had studied the whole population from which the sample was drawn).

Qualitative research also has a long tradition in the social and behavioral sciences, but has gained a large following in many applied fields only in recent decades. It is also easy to spot, first, because the titles of the articles will often contain the word "qualitative." In addition, qualitative researchers usually identify their research as qualitative in their introductions as well as in other parts of their reports.[3] You can also spot it because the results sections will be presented in terms of a narrative describing themes and trends—usually accompanied by quotations from the participants.

The literature on how to conduct qualitative research *emphasizes*:

1. Starting with a general problem without imposing rigid, specific purposes and hypotheses to guide the study. As data are collected on the problem, hypotheses may emerge, but they are subject to change as additional data are collected.
2. Selecting a purposive sample—not a random one. For example, a qualitative researcher may have access to some heroin addicts who attend a particular methadone clinic, and may believe that these clients of the clinic might provide useful insights into the problems of recovering addicts.[4]
3. Using a relatively small sample—sometimes as small as one exemplary case such as a mathematics teacher who has received a national award for teaching (once again, a purposive sample—selecting someone who might be useful for obtaining important information).
4. Measuring with relatively unstructured instruments such as semistructured interviews, unstructured observations, etc.
5. Measuring intensively (e.g., spending extended periods of time with the participants to gain in-depth insights into the phenomena of interest).
6. Presenting results mainly or exclusively in words with an emphasis on understanding the particular purposive sample studied and usually strongly de-emphasizing generalizations to larger populations.

As you can see by comparing the two lists above, the distinction between quantitative and qualitative research will be important when you evaluate studies for their strengths and weaknesses. For example, it is probably unfair to criticize a qualitative study for using only one classroom of 25 students when the researcher spent six months in the classroom observing and interacting with the students,

---

[3] Note that quantitative researchers rarely explicitly state that their research is quantitative.

[4] Note that a quantitative researcher might also study the clients of just one particular clinic to which she happens to have access. However, in the quantitative tradition, use of a sample of convenience such as the one in this example (as opposed to a random sample from a larger population) would be viewed as a serious flaw.

their parents, and the teacher to obtain detailed, in-depth information about them. (Note that it would be an exceptionally rare qualitative researcher who would have the resources to conduct such a study in hundreds of classrooms.) Still, you would want to make notes so that you can refer to the nature of this study in your literature review, as shown in Example 5.1.1. Notice that the reader has been informed that the study (a) is qualitative, (b) was intensive and long-term, and (c) involved only one classroom of 25 students. This is important background information for the readers, especially if you will be emphasizing this study in your review.

Example 5.1.1
Portion of a statement in a literature review:

Of the four qualitative studies on teacher-learner interactions in the classroom, Smith (1999) presents the most intensive, long-term study. In his study of 25 students in one classroom over a year, he found that….

On the other hand, a quantitative study in which forced-choice questionnaires mailed to all teachers in a large school district resulted in only 25 replies out of a potential 1,000 has an important weakness because those who responded may be presumed to be a biased sample of the population (e.g., perhaps only those who were interested in the topic of the questionnaire responded), making any generalizations to the population of 1,000 very risky. Notice that this weakness in the quantitative study is not offset by some parallel strength such as obtaining detailed in-depth information by studying the 25 students intensively, as would be done in a qualitative study.

✓ Guideline 2: Note whether a study is experimental or nonexperimental.

An *experimental* study is one in which treatments are administered to participants *for the purposes of the study* and their effects assessed. For example, in an experiment, some hyperactive students might be given Ritalin™ while others are given behavior therapy (such as systematic application of reward systems) in order to assess the relative effectiveness of the two treatments in reducing classroom discipline problems. Note that almost all experiments are quantitative.

A *nonexperimental* study is one in which participants' traits are measured without attempting to change them. For example, hyperactive students might be interviewed to understand their perceptions of their disruptive classroom behaviors without any attempt by the researcher to treat them. Such a study might be quantitative (if the researcher uses highly structured interview questions with choices for students to select from and summarizes the results statistically) or qualitative (if a researcher uses semistructured or unstructured interview questions[5] and uses words to summarize the results).

Here is an important caveat: Do not fall into the bad habit of referring to all empirical studies as experiments. For example, if you are reviewing nonexperimental studies, refer to them as "studies"—not "experiments." Use the term "experiment" only if treatments were given in order to observe their effects.

✔ Guideline 3: In an experiment, note whether the participants were assigned at random to treatment conditions.

An experiment in which participants are assigned at random to treatments is known as a *true experiment*. Random assignment guarantees that there is no bias in the assignment (i.e., with random assignment, there is no bias that would systematically assign the more disruptive students to the behavior therapy treatment while assigning the rest to be treated with Ritalin™). Other things being equal, more weight should be given to true experiments than to experiments using other methods of assignment such as using the students in one school as the experimental group and the students in another school as the control group. Note that students are not assigned schools at random. Hence, there may be important preexisting differences between the students in the two schools that may confound the interpretation of the results of such an experiment (e.g., socioeconomic status, language background, or self-selection, as occurs in "magnet" schools for the arts, the sciences, etc.).

✔ Guideline 4: Note attempts to examine cause-and-effect issues in nonexperimental studies.

The experimental method (with random assignment to treatment conditions) is widely regarded as the best quantitative method for investigating cause-and-effect issues. However, it is sometimes unethical, illegal, or administratively unfeasible to treat participants in certain ways. For example, if a researcher was exploring a possible causal link between the divorce of parents and their children dropping out of high school, it would be unethical to force some parents to get divorced while forcing others to remain married for the purposes of an experiment. For this research problem, the best that can be done is to obtain some students who have dropped out and some who have not dropped out but who are very similar in other important respects (such as socioeconomic status, the quality of the schools they attended, and so on) and then check to see if their parents' divorce rates differ in the hypothesized direction.[6] Suppose that the

---

[5] In addition, a qualitative researcher would be likely to conduct significantly longer interviews and, possibly, more than one interview.

[6] If the researcher had considerable resources and a long time frame, a prospective study could be conducted in which children are followed from the time they start school until they finish school, noting who drops out and who does not drop out as well as whose parents got divorced. This method is also

children of the divorced parents had somewhat higher drop-out rates than those of the children of nondivorced parents. Does this mean that divorce causes higher drop-out rates? Not necessarily. The conclusion is debatable because the researchers may have overlooked a number of other possible causal variables. Here is just one: Perhaps parents who tend to get divorced have poorer interpersonal skills and relate less well to their children. It may be this deficit in the children's upbringing (and not the divorce *per se*) that contributed to dropping out.[7]

The study we are considering is an example of a causal comparative study (or *ex post facto*) study. When using it, a researcher observes a current condition or outcome (such as dropping out) and searches the past for possible causal variables (such as divorce). Because causal comparative studies are considered to be more risky than true experiments for examining causality, you should note when a conclusion is based on the causal comparative method. In addition, you should consider whether there are other plausible causal interpretations that the researcher may have overlooked.

✓ Guideline 5: Note how the major variables were measured.

Most researchers directly address the issues of whether their measures are valid (i.e., measure what they claim to measure) and reliable (i.e., yield consistent results) in their research reports. However, many of them provide only brief information on these issues in their research reports. When they are brief, they often refer readers to other published sources of information on these characteristics of the measures they have used.[8] Other researchers provide extensive information on these matters, especially when they have used new measures designed for the research study on which they are reporting.

In either case, you should attempt to make preliminary assessments of whether the measures used seem appropriate for the research purpose. In addition, you should make notes on the types of measures used. This will allow you to make additional judgments when you review your notes in preparation for writing your literature review. As a general principle, if various researchers have used different methods of observation (e.g., questionnaires, observations, and interviews) and reached similar conclusions, these conclusions should be regarded as stronger than

---

inferior to the experimental method for identifying cause-and-effect relationships because of possible confounding (that is, many variables other than divorce may be responsible for the dropping out behavior, and the researchers may fail to control for them all).

[7] If this limitation is still not clear, consider the example further. Suppose an authoritarian government made it illegal for parents to divorce in order to reduce the dropout rate based on the study in question. If the real cause of dropping out was parents' poor interpersonal skills, preventing divorce would not have the presumed effect since it was misidentified as a causal agent. Instead, the government should have mounted programs to assist parents to improve their interpersonal skills, especially in dealing with their children.

[8] Note that quantitative researchers tend to call their measures "instruments."

conclusions based on various studies in which all the researchers used the same method of measurement.

Your notes might also reveal certain patterns that shed some light on discrepancies in results obtained by various researchers. For example, do all the studies that support a certain conclusion use one method of measurement while those that support a different conclusion use a different method? If your notes revealed this, you might consider making a statement such as the one in Example 5.5.1.

Example 5.5.1
A statement from a literature review that points out differences in measurement techniques (desirable):

While the two studies that used mailed questionnaires support the finding that inhalant use among adolescents is extremely rare, the three studies that used face-to-face interviews reported an incidence of more than 5%.

Note that Example 5.5.1 is much more informative than Example 5.5.2.

Example 5.5.2
A statement from a literature review that fails to point out differences in measurement techniques (undesirable):

The research on the incidence of adolescent inhalant use has yielded mixed results with two studies reporting that it is extremely rare and three others reporting an incidence of more than 5%.

✓ Guideline 6: Note the characteristics of the samples of participants.

As you learned in the first guideline in this chapter, quantitative and qualitative researchers have different perspectives on the selection of samples of participants. Without taking sides, it seems safe to say that if you plan to make generalizations in your literature review, you should make notes on whether the samples studied are likely to be representative of the populations to which one might wish to generalize. From quantitative researchers' point of view, random samples are best for this purpose.

Making notes on the demographics[9] of the participants can also help you identify patterns in the literature. For example, have the researchers who studied the transition from welfare to work using urban samples obtained different results from those who have studied rural samples? Could the differences in the urban-rural status of the participants (a demographic characteristic) help explain the differences in the findings? Note that you cannot answer such a question with certainty, but you could raise the possibility in your review. Other demographic

---

[9] Demographics are background characteristics of the participants.

characteristics often reported in research reports are gender, race/ethnicity, age, and socioeconomic status.

✓ Guideline 7:   Note how large a difference is—not just whether it is statistically significant.

When a researcher says a difference is statistically significant, he or she is reporting that a statistical test has indicated that the difference is greater than might be created by chance alone. It does *not* mean that the difference is necessarily large. It would take several chapters of a statistics textbook to explain the reasons why this is true. However, the following analogy may help you understand this point. Suppose there is a very tight race for the United States Senate, and Candidate A wins over Candidate B by 10 votes. This is, indeed, a very small difference, but it is quite significant, at least to the candidates (i.e., by counting all the votes systematically and carefully, we have identified a very small nonchance difference).

Given that even a small difference is often statistically significant, you will want to make note of the sizes of the differences you read about in the literature.[10] Suppose you read several studies that showed that computer-assisted instruction in English composition led to very slight, but statistically significant, increases in students' achievement. In fairness to your reader, you should point out the size of the differences as illustrated in Example 5.7.1. You will be prepared to write such statements if you make appropriate notes as you read and analyze the literature.

Example 5.7.1

In a series of true experiments at various colleges throughout the United States, the experimental groups receiving computer-assisted instruction consistently made very small but statistically significant greater gains than the control groups. On average, the gains were only about one percentage point on multiple-choice tests. These small gains make the use of experimental treatment on a widespread basis problematic because of the greatly increased cost of using it instead of the conventional (control) treatment.

✓ Guideline 8:   It is safe to presume that all empirical studies are flawed.

All empirical studies are subject to errors of various kinds, so no one study

---

[10] Increasingly, quantitative researchers are reporting a relatively new statistic called "effect size," which measures the size of a difference between groups of participants relative to the differences among individual participants. While a discussion of this statistic is beyond the scope of this book, should you encounter this statistic while reviewing literature, use this rough guideline: Effect sizes of less than about .25 indicate a small difference, and effect sizes above .50 indicate a large difference.

should be taken as providing the definitive answer(s) to a given research problem. In fact, that is why you are combing through the evidence reported in original reports of research—to weigh the various pieces of evidence, all of which are subject to error, to arrive at some reasonable conclusions based on a body of literature. This brings us to an important caveat: Never use the word "prove" when discussing the results of empirical research. Empirical studies do not prove anything. Instead they offer us degrees of evidence. While analyzing articles, make notes on how convincing the evidence is. Other things being equal, you will want to emphasize in your literature review the research articles that present the most convincing evidence. Thus, you should take more extensive notes on these studies than those that provide weak or questionable evidence.

This guideline leads us to another important principle. Namely, you will not be expected to dissect and discuss every flaw of every study you cite. Instead, you should make notes on major flaws, especially in studies that you plan to emphasize in your review. In addition, you should critique the methodology of studies in groups, whenever possible. For example, you might point out that all studies in a group you are reviewing have common weaknesses. Good note taking while you are reading the articles will help you identify such commonalties.

Concluding Comment

This short chapter briefly covers only some major methodological issues you might consider when you make notes in preparation for writing a review of literature. As you read the articles you have selected for your review, you will find additional information on these as well as other issues because researchers often critique the research of others in their literature reviews. In addition, many researchers include a section on the methodological limitations of their own studies in the Discussion sections of their reports.

Activities for Chapter 5

Directions: Locate an original report of empirical research, preferably on a topic you are reviewing, and answer the following questions. For learning purposes, your instructor may choose to assign an article for all students in your class to read.

1. Is the study you selected qualitative or quantitative? How did you make this determination?

2. Is the study experimental or nonexperimental? On what basis did you decide?

3. If the study is experimental, were the participants assigned at random to treatment conditions? If not, how were they assigned?

4. If it is nonexperimental, was the researcher attempting to examine cause-and-effect issues? If yes, did he or she use the causal comparative method? Explain.

5. What types of measures (i.e., instruments) were used? Did the researcher provide enough information about them to allow you to make judgments on their adequacy for use in the research? If yes, do you believe they were adequate in light of the information provided? If no, what types of additional information about the measures should have been reported?

6. Has the researcher described the demographics of the participants in sufficient detail? Explain.

7. If the researcher reported statistically significant differences, did he or she discuss whether they were large differences? In your opinion, are the differences large? Explain.

8. Briefly describe any major flaws in the research that you did not cover in your answers to questions 1 through 7.

Notes

Chapter 6

Synthesizing Literature Prior to Writing a Review

The guidelines in Chapters 4 and 5 have helped you to *conduct* the literature review. In other words, you have now read and analyzed a collection of research articles, and you have prepared detailed notes that describe discrete parts of these studies. You should now begin to synthesize these elements into a new whole, the sum of which will become your literature review.

The following guidelines will assist you in creating a basic framework within which you will report on the research you have reviewed. In other words, you are now ready to begin the process of *writing* the literature review. This chapter will help you develop an important product: a detailed writing outline.

✔ Guideline 1: Consider your purpose and voice before beginning to write.

Begin by asking yourself what your purpose is in writing a literature review. Are you trying to convince your professor that you have expended sufficient effort in preparing a term paper for your class? Are you trying to demonstrate your command of a field of study in a thesis or dissertation? Or, is your purpose to establish a context for a study you hope to have published in a journal? Each of these scenarios will result in a significantly different final product, in part because of the differences in the writer's purpose, but also because of differences in readers' expectations. Review the descriptions of these three types of literature reviews in Chapter 2, *Considerations in Writing Reviews for Specific Purposes.*

Once you establish your purpose and your audience, you can decide on an appropriate *voice*, or style of writing for your manuscript. You may know what you want to say, but how you say it will vary considerably if you are writing an e-mail message to a friend, a column for a newspaper, or a chapter in a thesis. A writer's voice, when preparing a literature review, should be formal because that is what the academic context dictates. The traditional *voice* in scientific writing dictates that the writer de-emphasize himself or herself in order to focus the readers' attention on the content. In Example 6.1.1, the writer's *self* is too much in evidence; it distracts the reader from the content of the statement. Example 6.1.2 is superior because it focuses on the content.

Example 6.1.1[1]
Improper "voice" for academic writing:

In this review, I will establish what I believe to be a major weakness in the literature on conflict resolution programs. Namely, my observation is that most of the evidence on the impact of the programs on various dependent variables is purely descriptive and anecdotal. I believe that broad claims such as "School mediation programs have proven themselves..."(Davis & Porter, 1985, p. 26) that are presented without supporting data may mislead readers, a misconception that I will try to rectify in this review. While reading the following review, you should keep in mind...

Example 6.1.2[2]
Suitable "voice" for academic writing:

The popularity of conflict resolution and peer mediation programs has resulted in numerous articles reporting claims about the programs' impact. The articles tend to provide (a) purely descriptive, anecdotal accounts of the programs' impact on various dependent variables (Davis & Porter, 1985; Edleson, 1981; Levy, 1989) and (b) descriptions of curriculum design and guidelines for developing a conflict resolution or peer mediation programs. Broad claims such as "School mediation programs have proven themselves..." (Davis & Porter, 1985, p. 26)...are presented but not supported by actual research data.

Notice that academic writers tend to avoid using the first person. Instead, they let the "facts" and arguments speak for themselves. This is not to say that the first person should never be used. It may be appropriate, for example, when relating a personal anecdote that graphically illustrates a point the writer is making. Example 6.1.3 illustrates this. Of course, personal anecdotes should be used sparingly and only when they are directly related to the topic at hand. For Example 6.1.3, the topic was "couples watching television," which is clearly related to the anecdote.

Example 6.1.3[3]

Five years ago, my parents bought a second television set because my mother refused to watch television with my father any longer. "I can't stand the way he flips through the channels," she said. Note that my father actually has the use of the new television, and my mother has been

---

[1] This is a hypothetical example.
[2] Johnson, D. W., & Johnson, R. T. (1996). Conflict resolution and peer mediation programs in the elementary and secondary school: A review of the research. *Review of Educational Research, 66,* 459–506 (p. 461).
[3] Walker, A. J. (1996). Couples watching television: Gender, power and the remote control. *Journal of Marriage and the Family, 58,* 813–823 (p. 813).

relegated to the den with the older model. Nevertheless, mother now has her own set, and conflicts about the remote control device have been reduced considerably.

✔ Guideline 2:   Consider how to reassemble your notes.

Now that you have established your purpose for writing your review, identified your audience, and established your voice, you should reevaluate your notes to determine how the pieces you have described will be reassembled. At the outset, you should recognize that it is generally unacceptable in writing a literature review to present a series of annotations of research studies. That would be, in essence, like describing trees when you really should be describing a forest. In the case of a literature review, you are creating a unique new forest, which you will build by using the trees you found in the literature you have read. In order to build this new whole, you should consider how the pieces relate to one another while preparing a topic outline, which is described in more detail under the next guideline.

✔ Guideline 3:   Create a topic outline that traces your "argument."

Like any other kind of essay, the review should *first* establish for the reader the line of argumentation you will follow (this is called the *thesis* in composition classes). This can be stated in the form of an assertion, a contention or a proposition; *then*, the writer should develop a traceable narrative that demonstrates that the line of argumentation is worthwhile and justified. This means that the writer should have formed judgments about the topic based on the analysis and synthesis of the research literature.

The topic outline should be designed as a kind of road map of the argument, which is illustrated in Example 6.3.1. Notice that it starts with an assertion (that there is a severe shortage of donor organs and that understanding the psychological components of donation decisions could help to address the shortage). Then the introduction is followed by a systematic review of the relevant areas of the research literature and ends with a conclusion that relates back to the original assertion. Since this outline will be referred to at various points throughout the rest of this chapter, please take a moment to examine it carefully. Place a flag on the next page or bookmark it for easy reference to the outline when you are referred to it later.

Example 6.3.1[4]

Sample topic outline:

Topic: Psychological Aspects of Organ Donation: Individual and Next-of-Kin Donation Decisions

I. Introduction
    A. Establish importance of the topic (cite statistics on scarcity of organs).
    B. Delimit the review to psychological components of decisions.
    C. Describe organization of the paper, indicating that the remaining topics in the outline will be discussed.

II. Individual decisions regarding posthumous organ donation
    A. Beliefs about organ donation.
    B. Attitudes toward donating.
    C. Stated willingness to donate.
    D. Summary of research on individual decisions.

III. Next-of-kin consent decisions
    A. Beliefs about donating others' organs.
    B. Attitudes toward next-of-kin donations.
    C. Summary of research on next-of-kin consent decisions.

IV. Methodological issues and directions for future research
    A. Improvement in attitude measures and measurement strategy.
    B. Greater differentiation by type of donation.
    C. Stronger theoretical emphasis.
    D. Greater interdisciplinary focus.

V. Summary, Conclusions, and Implications
    A. Summary of points I–IV.
    B. Need well-developed theoretical models of attitudes and decision making.
    C. Current survey data limited in scope and application points to need for more sophisticated research in the future.
    D. Need more use of sophisticated data analytic techniques.
    E. Conclusion: Psychology can draw from various subdisciplines for an understanding of donation decisions so intervention strategies can be identified. Desperately need to increase the available supply of donor organs.

✓ Guideline 4: Reorganize your notes according to the path of your argument.

The topic outline described in the previous step describes the path of the authors' argument. The next step is to reorganize the notes according to the outline. Begin by coding the notes with references to the appropriate places in the outline. For example, on the actual note cards write a "I" beside notations that cite statistics on the scarcity of donated organs, a "II" beside notations that deal with individual decisions about organ donations, a "III" beside notations that deal with next-of-kin decisions, and a "IV" beside notations that pertain to methodological issues. Then return to the topic outline and indicate the specific references to

---

[4] The outline is based on the work of Radicki, C.M., & Jaccard, J. (1997). Psychological aspects of organ donation: A critical review and synthesis of individual and next-of-kin donation decisions. *Health Psychology, 16*, 183-195.

particular studies. For example, if Doe & Smith (1999) cite statistics on the scarcity of donated organs, write their names on the outline to the right of point number I.

✓ Guideline 5: Within each topic heading, note relationships among studies.

The next step is to note on your topic outline the relationships among studies. One type of relationship you will almost always want to consider is whether it is possible to group the articles into subtopics. For example, for "Beliefs about organ donation" (point IIA in Example 6.3.1), the literature can be grouped into the five subcategories in Example 6.5.1.

Example 6.5.1
Additional subtopics for point IIA in Example 6.3.1

1. Religious beliefs
2. Cultural beliefs
3. Knowledge (i.e., beliefs based on "facts" people have gathered from a variety of sources)
4. Altruistic beliefs
5. Normative beliefs (i.e., beliefs based on perceptions of what is acceptable within a particular social group)

These would become subtopics under point IIA ("Beliefs about organ donation") in the topic outline. In other words, your outline will become more detailed as you identify additional subtopics.

The other type of relationship you will want to consider is the consistency of results from study to study. For example, the reviewers on whose work Example 6.3.1 is based found three articles suggesting that there are cultural obstacles that reduce the number of organ donations among Hispanics, while one other article indicated a willingness to donate and a high level of awareness about transplantation issues among this group. When you discuss such discrepancies, assist your reader by providing relevant information about the research, with an eye to identifying possible explanations for the differences. Were the first three articles older and the last one more current? Did the first three use a different methodology for collecting the data (e.g., did those with the negative results examine hospital records while the one with a positive result use self-report questionnaires)? Noting differences such as these may give you interesting issues to raise when you write your literature review.

✓ Guideline 6:   Within each topic heading, look for obvious gaps or areas needing more research.

The reviewers of the topic in Example 6.3.1 noted that whereas much cross-cultural research has been conducted on African Americans, Asian Americans, and Hispanics, only a few studies have focused on Native Americans—a fact that a writer might want to mention in a review of research when discussing cultural beliefs.

✓ Guideline 7:   Plan to discuss how individual studies relate to and advance theory.

The importance of theoretical literature was discussed in Chapter 1. You should consider how individual studies, which are often narrow, help define, illustrate, or advance theoretical notions. Often, researchers will point out how their studies relate to theory, which will help you in your considerations of this matter. Specify that theory will be discussed in your literature review by including it in your topic outline, which was done in point VB in Example 6.3.1, which indicates that the reviewer will discuss the need for well-defined theoretical models.

If there are competing theories in your area, plan to discuss the extent to which the literature you have reviewed supports each of them, keeping in mind that an inconsistency between the results of a study and a prediction based on theory may result from *either* imperfections in the theoretical model or imperfections in the research methodology used in the study.

✓ Guideline 8:   Plan to summarize periodically and, again, near the end of the review.

It is helpful to summarize the inferences, generalizations, and/or conclusions you have drawn from your review of the literature in stages. For instance, the outline in Example 6.3.1 calls for summaries at two intermediate points in the literature review (i.e., points IID and IIIC). Long, complex topics within a literature review often deserve their own separate summaries. These summaries help readers to understand the direction the author is taking and invite readers to pause, think about, and internalize difficult material.

You have probably already noticed that the last main topic (Topic V) in Example 6.3.1 calls for a summary of all the material that preceded it. It is usually appropriate to start the last section of a long review with a summary of the main points already covered. This shows readers what the writer views as the major points and sets the stage for a discussion of the writer's conclusions and any implications he or she has drawn.

✔ Guideline 9: Plan to present conclusions and implications.

Note that a *conclusion* is a statement about the state of the knowledge on a topic. Example 6.9.1 illustrates a conclusion. Note that it does not say that there is "proof." Reviewers should hedge and talk about degrees of evidence (e.g., "it seems safe to conclude" or "one conclusion might be").

Example 6.9.1[5]

In light of the research on cultural differences in attitudes toward organ donation, *it seems safe to conclude* (emphasis added) that cultural groups differ substantially in their attitudes toward organ donation and that effective intervention strategies need to take account of these differences. Specifically,...

If the weight of the evidence on a topic does not clearly favor one conclusion over the other, be prepared to say so. Example 6.9.2 illustrates this technique.

Example 6.9.2

Although the majority of the studies indicate Method A is superior, several methodologically strong studies point to the superiority of Method B. In the absence of additional evidence, *it is difficult to conclude* (emphasis added)...

An *implication* is usually a statement of what people or organizations should do in light of existing research. In other words, a reviewer usually should make suggestions as to what actions seem promising based on the review of the research. Thus, it is usually desirable to include the term "implications" near the end of a topic outline. Example 6.9.3 is an implication because it suggests that a particular intervention might be effectively used with a particular group.

Example 6.9.3

The body of evidence reviewed in this paper suggests that when working with Asian Americans, Intervention A seems most promising for increasing the number of organ donations made by this group.

At first, some novice writers feel that they should describe only "facts" from the published research and not venture on to offer their own conclusions and implications. Keep in mind, however, that a person who has done a thorough and careful job of reviewing the literature on a topic has, in fact, become an expert on it. To whom else should we look for advice on the state of a knowledge base

---

[5] The three examples for this guideline are hypothetical.

(conclusions) and what we should do to be more effective (implications) than an expert who is up-to-date on the research on a topic?

✓ Guideline 10: Plan to suggest directions for future research at the end of your review.

Note that in Example 6.3.1, the reviewer plans to discuss future research under point V. As you plan what to say, keep in mind that it is inadequate to simply suggest that "more research is needed in the future." Instead, you should make specific suggestions. For instance, if all (or almost all the researchers) have used self-report questionnaires, you might call for future research using other means of data collection. If there are understudied groups such as Native Americans, you might call for more research on them. If almost all the studies are quantitative, you might call for additional qualitative studies. The list of possibilities is almost endless. Your job is to suggest those that you think are most promising for advancing knowledge in the area you are reviewing.

✓ Guideline 11: Flesh out your outline with details from your analysis.

Now comes the final step before you will begin to write your first draft. You should go back over your outline and flesh it out with specific details from your analysis of the research literature. Make every effort, as you expand the outline, to include enough details to be able to write clearly about the studies you are including. Make sure to note the strengths and weaknesses of studies as well as the gaps, relationships, and major trends or patterns that emerge in the literature. At the end of this step, your outline will be several pages in length, and you will be ready to write your first draft.

Example 6.11.1 illustrates how a small portion of the topic outline in Example 6.3.1 (point IIA) would look if it were fleshed out with additional details.

Example 6.11.1

Part of a fleshed-out outline
II. Individual decisions regarding posthumous organ donation
   A. Beliefs about organ donation (research can be categorized into 5 major groupings)
      1. Religious beliefs
         a. Define the term "religious beliefs"
         b. Religions that support organ donation
            (1) Buddhism, Hindu (Ulshafer, 1988; Woo, 1992)
            (2) Catholicism (Ulshafer, 1988)
            (3) Judaism (Bulka, 1990; Cohen, 1988; Pearl, 1990; Weiss, 1988)
            (4) Protestantism (Walters, 1988)
            (5) Islam (Gatrad, 1994; Rispler-Chaim, 1989; Sachedina, 1988)
         c. Religions that do not support it
            (1) Jehovah's Witnesses (Corlett, 1985; Pearl, 1990)
            (2) Orthodox Judaism (Corlett, 1985; Pearl, 1990)
         d. Other sources that have commented on religion as a barrier (Basu et al., 1989; Gallup Organization, 1993; Moores et al., 1976)

Notice that several of the references in Example 6.11.1 appear in more than one place. For instance, Corlett's 1985 report will be referred to under a discussion of both Jehovah's Witnesses and Orthodox Judaism. This is appropriate because a reviewer should *not* be writing a series of summaries in which Corlett's study is summarized in one place and then dropped. Instead, it should be cited as many times as needed, depending on how many specific points in the outline it bears on.

Activities for Chapter 6

Directions: Refer to the three review articles in the Supplementary Readings section near the end of this book while answering the following questions.

1. Reread Review Article A in the Supplementary Readings section, "Individual Differences in Student Cheating," and develop a topical outline for it.
   - What categories were used by the authors to group the articles they reviewed?
   - Describe one case in which the authors have identified a gap in the literature.
   - Note another example in which the authors explicitly comment about other kinds of relationships between studies (i.e., similarities, differences, etc.).

2. For each of the three reviews, answer the following questions.
   - Do the writers use an academic or a casual "voice?"
   - Is their writing formal or informal?
   - Which one of the three reviews is the most casual?
   - Which reviews are written in a formal style?

3. Consider again Review Article A in the Supplementary Readings. In a paragraph, describe the authors' main points. In your opinion, have these points been made effectively? Explain.

Notes

Chapter 7

Guidelines for Writing a First Draft

Let us review what you have accomplished thus far. You have conducted a thorough literature review by searching for research articles in your area of study, by making careful notes of specific details of these studies, and by analyzing these details to identify patterns, relationships among studies, gaps in the body of literature, as well as strengths and weaknesses in particular studies. Then, in Chapter 6, you reorganized your notes and developed a detailed writing outline as you prepared yourself to begin to write your literature review.

In other words, you have already completed the most difficult steps in the writing process: the analysis and synthesis of the literature and the charting of the course of your argument. These preliminary steps constitute the intellectual process of preparing a literature review. The remaining steps—drafting, editing, and redrafting—will now require you to translate the results of your intellectual labor into a narrative account of what you have found.

The guidelines in this chapter will help you to produce the main product of this chapter, a first draft of your literature review. The guidelines in Chapter 8 will help you to develop a coherent essay and avoid producing a series of annotations, and Chapter 9 will present additional guidelines that relate to style, mechanics, and language usage.

✔ Guideline 1: Identify the broad problem area, but avoid global statements.

In general, the introduction of a literature review should begin with the identification of the broad problem area under review. The rule of thumb is, "Go from the general to the specific." However, there are limits on how general to be in the beginning. Consider Example 7.1.1. As the beginning of a literature review on a topic in education, it is much too broad. It fails to identify any particular area or topic. You should avoid starting your review with such global statements.

Example 7.1.1
Beginning of a literature review in education that is too broad:

Education is important to both the economy of the United States and to the rest of the world. Without education, students will be unprepared for the next millenium....

Contrast Example 7.1.1 with Example 7.1.2, which is also on a topic in education but clearly relates to the specific topic that will be reviewed: studies of educational tutoring.

Example 7.1.2[1]

Beginning of a literature review in education that is sufficiently specific:

Human tutoring provided on a one-to-one basis has been credited as the most effective form of instruction (Bloom, 1984; Cohen, Kulik, & Kulik, 1982). It is not surprising then, that efforts to isolate and describe the actions of expert tutors and the unique interactions that take place between tutor and tutee have intensified....

✓ Guideline 2: Indicate clearly why certain studies are important.

If you believe a particular study is important, state clearly why you think so. For instance, the author of Example 7.2.1 identifies a study as the "most comprehensive," thereby indicating its importance.

Example 7.2.1[2]

According to the *most comprehensive study* (emphasis added) to date (MacKenzie et al., 1995), based on a comparative analysis of programs in eight states, no clear-cut statements can...

A study may also be important because it represents a pivotal point in the development of an area of research, such as an article that represents a reversal of an author's position or one that has launched a new methodology. These and other characteristics of a study may justify its status as an important study. Make sure your review makes this clear for the reader.

✓ Guideline 3: If you are commenting on the timeliness of a topic, be specific in describing the time frame.

Avoid beginning your review with unspecific references to the timeliness of a topic, as in, "In recent years, there has been an increased interest in...." This beginning would leave many questions unanswered for the reader. What years are being referenced? How did the writer determine that the "interest" is increasing? Who has become more interested, the writer or others in the field? Is it possible that the writer became interested in the topic recently while others have been losing interest?

---

[1] Derry, S. J. & Potts, M. K. (1998). How tutors model students: A study of personal constructs in adaptive tutoring. *American Educational Research Journal, 35,* 65–99, p. 66.

[2] Zhang, S. X. (1998). In search of hopeful glimpses: A critique of research strategies in current boot camp evaluations. *Crime & Delinquency, 44*(2), 314-334, p. 315.

The authors of Example 7.3.1 avoided such problems in interpretation by naming the years and citing statistics that show an increase in a problem. If statistics such as these are not available for your topic, you should probably omit references to the currency of the problem because you would lack the factual basis for making the statement.

Example 7.3.1[3]

Child maltreatment incident reports increased by 50% *between 1988 and 1993* (emphasis added), totaling more than 2.9 million reports in 1993 (McCurdy & Daro, 1994). Much of this increase can be attributed to substance abuse (Curtis & McCullough, 1993; General Accounting Office, 1994; McCurdy & Daro, 1994; Tatara, 1989-1990). (p. 393)

✓ Guideline 4: If citing a classic or landmark study, identify it as such.

Make sure that you identify the classic or landmark studies in your review. Such studies are often pivotal points in the historical development of the published literature. In addition, they are also often responsible for framing a particular question or a research tradition. In addition, they may be the original source of key concepts or terminology used in the subsequent literature. Whatever their contribution, you should identify their status as classics or landmarks in the literature. Consider Example 7.4.1, in which a landmark (first of its kind) study is cited.

Example 7.4.1[4]

The *first content analysis* (emphasis added) of gender biases in magazine advertisements was published by Courtney and Lockeretz (1971). Those authors found that magazine advertisements reflected four general stereotypes: (a) "A woman's place is in the home," (b) "Women do not make important decisions or do important things," (c) "Women are dependent and need men's protection," and (d) "Men regard women primarily as sex objects; they are not interested in women as people." (p. 628)

✓ Guideline 5: If a landmark study was replicated, mention that and indicate the results of the replication.

As noted in the previous guideline, landmark studies typically stimulate additional research. In fact, many are replicated a number of times, using different

---

[3] Akin, B. A., Gregoire, T. K. (1997). Parents' views on child welfare's response to addiction. *Journal of Contemporary Human Services, 78*(4), 393-404.

[4] Neptune, D. & Plous, S. (1997). Racial and gender biases in magazine advertising. *Psychology of Women Quarterly, 21*, 627-644.

groups of participants or by adjusting other research design variables. If you are citing a landmark study and it has been replicated, you should mention that fact and indicate whether the replications were successful. This is illustrated in Example 7.5.1, which is an elaboration on Example 7.4.1.

Example 7.5.1

Since the time of this study, a number of *other content analyses have replicated these results* (emphasis added) (Belkaoui & Belkaoui, 1976; Busby & Leichty, 1993; Culley & Bennett, 1976; England, Kuhn & Gardner, 1983; Lysonski, 1983; Sexton & Haberman, 1974; Venkatesan & Losco, 1975; Wagner & Banos, 1973). During the past 40 years, only one of the stereotypes found by Courtney and Lockeretz (1971) has shown evidence of amelioration: the image of women as homebound. As women have entered the workforce in growing numbers, advertisements have increasingly shown them in work settings outside the home (Busby & Leichty, 1993; Sullivan & O'Connor, 1988). (p. 628)

✔ Guideline 6: Discuss other literature reviews on your topic.

If you find an earlier published review on your topic, it is important to discuss it in your review. Before doing so, consider the following questions:

How is the other review different from yours?
 Is yours substantially more current?
 Did you delimit the topic in a different way?
 Did you conduct a more comprehensive review?
 Did the earlier reviewer reach the same major conclusions that you reached?

How worthy is the other review of your readers' attention?
 What will they gain, if anything, by reading it?
 Will they encounter a different and potentially helpful perspective on the problem area?

✔ Guideline 7: Refer the reader to other reviews on issues that you will not be discussing in detail.

If you find it necessary to refer to a *related issue* that cannot be covered in depth in your review, it is appropriate to refer the reader to other reviews, as in Example 7.7.1. Needless to say, your review should completely cover the specific topic you have chosen. It is not acceptable to describe just a portion of the literature on your topic (as you defined it) and then refer the reader to another source for the remainder.

Example 7.7.1[5]

This instrument, originally created by criminologists from 15 Western countries, has gone through a series of empirical tests and is now considered methodologically sound (for a detailed discussion of it, see Junger-Tas, Terlouw, and Klein 1994). In addition, it... (p. 323)

✓ Guideline 8: Justify comments such as "no studies were found."

If you find a gap in the literature that deserves mention in your literature review, explain how you arrived at the conclusion that there is a gap. At the very least, explain how you conducted the literature search, which databases you searched, and the dates and other parameters you used. You do not need to be overly specific, but the reader will expect you to justify your statement about the gap.

To avoid misleading readers, it is a good idea to make statements such as the one shown in Example 7.8.1. early on in your review. This will protect you from criticism if you point out a gap when one does not actually exist. In other words, you are telling your reader that there is a gap based on the use of *a particular search strategy.*

Example 7.8.1[6]

The studies used in this meta-analysis were located via a comprehensive search of the literature. Electronic searches were performed on the ERIC (1966-1994), PsycLIT (1974-1994), Sociofile (1974-1994), Dissertation Abstracts (1965-1994), and Social Sciences Citation Index (1989-1994) databases. Although the search strategy varied depending on the database, search terms included group composition, grouping for instructional purposes, small group, team learning, team instruction, hetero-geneous/homogeneous grouping, group structure, ability grouping, peer tutoring, and cooperative learning. Through branching from primary studies and review articles, other citations were found and included. In total, the search uncovered over 3,000 published articles concerning within-class grouping. (p. 429)

✓ Guideline 9: Avoid long lists of nonspecific references.

In academic writing, references are used in the text of a written document for at least two purposes. First, they are used to give proper credit to an author of an idea or, in the case of a direct quotation, of a specific set of words. A failure to

---

[5] Zhang, S. X. (1998). In search of hopeful glimpses: A critique of research strategies in current boot camp evaluations. *Crime & Delinquency, 44,* 314-334.

[6] Lou, Y., Abrami, P. C., Spence, J.C., Poulsen, C., Chambers, B., & d'Apollonia, S. (1996). Within-class grouping: A meta-analysis. *Review of Educational Research, 66*(4), 423-458.

do so would constitute plagiarism. Second, references are used to demonstrate the breadth of coverage given in a manuscript. In an introductory paragraph, for example, it may be desirable to include references to several key studies that will be discussed in more detail in the body of the review. However, it is inadvisable to use long lists of references that do not specifically relate to the point being expressed. For instance, in Example 7.9.1, the long list of nonspecific references in the first sentence is probably inappropriate. Are these all empirical studies? Do they report their authors' speculations on the issue? Are some of the references more important than others? It would have been better for the authors to refer the reader to a few key studies, which themselves would contain references to additional examples of research in that particular area, which is illustrated in Example 7.9.2.

Example 7.9.1
First sentence in a literature review (too many nonspecific references):

Numerous writers have indicated that children in single-parent households are at greater risk for academic underachievement than children from two-parent households (Adams, 1991; Block, 1992; Doe, 1996; Edgar, 1999; Hampton, 1995; Jones, 1998, Klinger, 1991; Long, 1992; Livingston, 1993; Macy, 1985; Norton, 1988; Pearl, 1994; Smith, 1996; Travers, 1997; Vincent, 1994; West, 1992; Westerly, 1995; and Yardley, 1999).

Example 7.9.2
An improved version of Example 7.9.1:

Numerous writers have suggested that children in single-parent households are at greater risk for academic underachievement than children from two-parent households (see, for example, Adams, 1991 and Block, 1992). Three recent studies have provided strong empirical support for this contention (Doe, 1996, Edgar, 1999, and Jones, 1998). Of these, the study by Jones is the strongest, employing a national sample with rigorous controls for....

Notice the use of "see, for example," which indicates that only some of the possible references are cited for the point that the writers "have suggested." You may also use the Latin abbreviation *cf.* (which means "compare").

✔ Guideline 10: If the results of previous studies are inconsistent or widely varying, cite them separately.

It is not uncommon for studies on the same topic to produce inconsistent or widely varying results. If so, it is important to cite the studies separately in order for the reader to interpret your review correctly. The following two examples illustrate the potential problem. Example 7.10.1 is misleading because it fails to note that the previous studies are grouped according to the two extremes of the percentage range given. Example 7.10.2 illustrates a better way to cite inconsistent findings.

Example 7.10.1
Inconsistent results cited as a single finding (undesirable):

Previous studies have found anywhere from 39% to 68% of college students reporting intervening in an intoxicated driving intervention (Mills & McCarty, 1983; Rabow, Hernandez, & Watts, 1986; Hernandez, Newcomb, & Rabow, 1995).

Example 7.10.2[7]
Improved version of Example 7.10.1

Previous studies have found anywhere from 39% of college students (Mills & McCarty, 1983; Rabow, Hernandez, & Watts, 1986) to 68% of college students (Hernandez, Newcomb, & Rabow, 1995) reporting intervening in an intoxicated driving intervention. (p. 4)

✔ Guideline 11: Cite all relevant references in the review section of a thesis, dissertation, or journal article.

When writing a thesis, a dissertation, or an article for publication, in which the literature review precedes a report of original research, you should usually first cite all the relevant references in the literature review of your document. Avoid introducing new references to literature in later sections such as the results or discussion sections. Make sure you have checked your entire document to ensure that the literature review section or chapter is comprehensive. You may refer back to a previous discussion of a pertinent study when discussing your conclusions, but the study should have been referenced first in the literature review at the beginning of the thesis, dissertation, or article.

✔ Guideline 12: Emphasize the need for your study in the literature review section or chapter.

When writing a thesis, a dissertation, or an article for publication, in which the literature review precedes a report of original research, you should use the review to help justify your study. You can do this in a variety of ways, such as pointing out that your study (1) closes a gap in the literature, (2) tests an important aspect of a current theory, (3) replicates an important study, (4) retests a

---

[7] Drucker, A. D. & Powell, J. L. (1997). The role of peer conformity in the decision to ride with an intoxicated driver. *Journal of Alcohol and Drug Education, 43*(1), 1-7.

hypothesis using new or improved methodological procedures, or (5) is designed to resolve conflicts in the literature, and so on.

Example 7.12.1 was included in the literature review portion of a study designed to explore the stressors experienced by Black men following divorce and the strategies they use to cope with divorce. By pointing out the potential problem and the lack of relevant research, the researchers have established the need for their study.

Example 7.12.1[8]

Despite the high rate of marital dissolution among Blacks, there is an absence of studies that have examined Black men's divorce experience. This lack of research is surprising because marital dissolution has been characterized as a particularly stressful process for Black men (Albrecht, 1980....

In Example 7.12.2, the researchers help establish the need for their observational study of preschool children by citing literature suggesting there are insufficient observational studies of this group and noting the benefits of observation, which helps to justify the need for their study.

Example 7.12.2[9]

Scales et al. (1991) further indicate that there is a relative lack of observational studies of preschool children's behavior in group settings. Observational studies, while difficult to conduct, afford insights into and examination of complex social interactions.

Activities for Chapter 7

1. Reread Review Article A in Supplementary Readings, "Individual Differences in Student Cheating."
   - How did the authors indicate the importance of the topic of their review?
   - Locate three places in the review where the authors emphasized the need for research of the type they have undertaken.

2. Reread Review Article C in Supplementary Readings, "Immune Neglect: A Source of Durability Bias in Affective Forecasting."

---

[8] Lawson, E. J. & Thomson, A. (1996). Black men's perceptions of divorce-related stressors and strategies for coping with divorce. *Journal of Family Issues, 17,* 249–273, p. 250.
[9] Bagley, D. M. & Klass, D. M. (1997). Comparison of the quality of preschoolers' play in housekeeping and thematic sociodramatic play centers. Journal of Research in Childhood Education, 12, 71-77, p. 72.

- What function does the opening quotation play in the review?
- What function do the first two paragraphs play in the review?

3. Locate the introductions for all three review articles in Supplementary Readings.
   - Which of the three introductions is the most complex? Why do you think the authors made the introduction so complex?
   - Which of the three introductions was the easiest to comprehend? Explain.

Notes

Chapter 8

Guidelines for Developing a Coherent Essay

This chapter is designed to help you to refine your first draft by guiding you in developing a coherent essay. Remember that a literature review should not be written as a series of connected summaries (or annotations) of the several articles you have read. Instead, the review should have a clearly stated argument, and it should be developed in such a way that all of its elements work together to communicate a well-reasoned account of that argument.

✓ Guideline 1: Describe the outline of your review for the reader.

An effective literature review often is a synthesis of research from more than one specific field or area of study. In other words, you can fairly well predict that your readers will be unfamiliar with some of the work you will cover, even if they are from your discipline area. However, even if they are familiar with the literature, your synthesis will be providing a unique interpretation, which your readers should be able to grasp quickly. For these reasons, it is important in academic writing to provide your readers with an explicit road map of your argument. This is usually done in the introductory section of the review, which should include an overview of what will be covered in the rest of the document. Example 8.1.1 illustrates this.

Example 8.1.1[1]
An effective "road map" at the beginning of a review:
This article provides an overview of the literature that reveals extensive classifications of the family secret. The review includes definitions, comparisons of family secrecy to family privacy, types of family secrets, reasons why families avoid exposing certain activities, and factors contributing to the maintenance of a secret. The disclosing of hidden information is discussed, with emphasis on how such revelations occur, factors influencing exposition as well as the functions, and negative consequences of such openness. The article concludes with suggestions for further research. (p. 22)

---

[1] Brown-Smith, N. (1998). Family secrets. *Journal of Family Issues, 19*(1), 20-42.

✓ Guideline 2:   Near the beginning of a review, state explicitly what will and will not be covered.

Some topics are so broad that it will not be possible for you to cover the research completely in your review, especially if you are writing a term paper, which may have page-length restrictions imposed by your instructor, or an article for publication, in which reviews traditionally are relatively short. In such cases, you should state explicitly, near the beginning of your review, what will and will not be covered (i.e., the delimitations of your review). The excerpt in Example 8.2.1 illustrates application of this guideline.

Example 8.2.1[2]

To accomplish this goal, a comprehensive literature review of current boot camp evaluations was conducted. However, the review was by no means exhaustive. The numerous internal studies conducted by boot camp administering agencies were not included here because it would be difficult to select a representative range of these publications. Therefore, readers need to take into account the limited scope of this literature search, which focused on published studies involving primary data collections. (p. 316)

✓ Guideline 3:   Specify your point of view early in the review.

As has been emphasized previously, your literature review should be written in the form of an essay that has a particular point of view in looking at the reviewed research. This point of view serves as the thesis statement of your essay, the assertion or proposition that is supported in the remainder of the essay. This statement can be as simple as the assertion that research with alternative populations will shed light on your topic. On the other hand, your review may have a more complex proposition. Either way, you need to articulate the point of your essay. Therefore, when you begin to write, you should establish your point of view early in the review so your readers can follow your argument.

One way of doing this is to incorporate your point of view into the description of the path of your argument in your introductory statements. In other words, state explicitly what your intention for writing the review was as part of your description of the contents of your paper. This can be especially helpful if your review is long and complex. Example 8.3.1 illustrates this technique.

---

[2] Zhang, S.X. (1998). In search of hopeful glimpses: A critique of research strategies in current boot camp evaluations. *Crime & Delinquency, 44,* 314-334.

Example 8.3.1[3]
Early summary of the path of an argument:

Our goal in this article is to determine the conditions under which the social environment beneficially influences adjustment to cancer. We review studies that examine the effect of the social environment on psychological adjustment, and we include the very small literature on the role of the social environment in the progression of disease.

✔ Guideline 4: Aim for a clear and cohesive essay; avoid annotations.

It has been emphasized several times thus far that an effective literature review should be written in the form of an essay. Perhaps the single most-reported problem for novice academic writers is their difficulty in abandoning the use of annotations in the body of a literature review.

Annotations are brief summaries of the contents of articles. Stringing together several annotations in the body of a review may describe what research is available on a topic, but it fails to organize the material for the reader. An effective review of literature is organized to make a point. The writer needs to describe how the individual studies relate to one another. What are the relative strengths and weaknesses? Where are the gaps, and why do they exist? All these details and more need to support the author's main purpose for writing the review. The detailed outline developed in Chapter 6 describes the path of the argument, but it is up to the writer to translate this into a prose account that integrates the important details of the research literature into an essay that communicates a point of view.

Example 8.4.1 shows how a number of studies can be cited together as part of an essay, with citations for each of the two main points in the paragraph.

Example 8.4.1[4]

Although some researchers have concluded that increased social contact does increase expressed acceptance of students with mental retardation (Peterson, 1974; Sheare, 1974), the bulk of the data (Balter & Smith, 1981; Cook & Wollersheim, 1976; Goodman et al., 1972;…Janney, Snell, Beers, & Raynes, 1995; Strauch, 1970) suggests that integration alone does not enhance typical children's attitudes toward their peers with mental retardation.

---

[3] Helgeson, V. S. & Cohen, S. (1996). Social support and adjustment to cancer: Reconciling descriptive, correlational, and intervention research. *Health Psychology, 15,* 135-148, p. 136.

[4] Hammond, D. G., Zucker, S. H., Burstein, K. S., & De Gangi, S. A. (1997). Computer mediated instruction for increasing regular education students' acceptance of students with mental retardation. *Education and Training in Mental Retardation and Developmental Disabilities, 32,* 313-320, p. 314.

✔ Guideline 5: Use subheadings, especially in long reviews.

Because long reviews, especially those written for theses and dissertations, often deal with articles from more than one discipline area, it is advisable to use subheadings. If you decide to use subheadings, place them strategically to help advance your argument and allow the reader to follow your discussion more easily. The topic outline you prepared in Chapter 6 can help you to determine where they should be placed, though you may need to recast some of the topic headings as labels rather than statements.

✔ Guideline 6: Use transitions to help trace your argument.

Strategic transitional phrases can help readers follow your argument. For instance, you can use transitions to provide the reader with textual clues that mark the progression of a discussion, such as when you begin paragraphs with "First," "Second," and "Third" to mark the development of three related points. Of course, any standard writing manual will contain lists of transitional expressions that are commonly used in formal writing.

These transitions should not be overused, however. Especially in a short review, it may not be necessary to use such phrases to label the development of three related points when each is described in three adjacent paragraphs. Another problem often found in short reviews is the overuse of what Bem (1995)[5] calls "meta-comments," which are comments about the review *itself* (as opposed to comments about the literature being reviewed). For instance, in Example 8.6.1, the writer restates the organization of the review (i.e., this is an example of a meta-comment) partway through the document. While there is nothing inherently wrong with making meta-comments, you should avoid frequent restatements that rehash what you have already stated.

Example 8.6.1
Example of overuse of meta-comments:

Recall that this paper deals with how question-asking in children has been used to explain a variety of learning styles. Also recall that we have reviewed the research on the use of question-asking in the classroom and have reached some tentative conclusions regarding its conclusions. Now, we will consider two basic types of questions that young children frequently ask, noting that...

---

[5] Bem, D. J. (1995). Writing a review article for *Psychological Bulletin. Psychological Bulletin, 118*(2), 172-177.

✔ Guideline 7: Consider preparing a table that compares important characteristics of the studies reviewed.

It is sometimes useful to prepare a table that displays the main characteristics of the studies you have reviewed, especially if the research you have reviewed is of a single type. For instance, the table in Example 8.7.1 describes the important characteristics of a set of related studies. Such tables are especially helpful when there are many studies to be covered in a review. Despite the presentation of such a table, the writer of a review is still obligated to discuss in paragraph form at least the more important studies cited.

Example 8.7.1
Small portion of a table summarizing many studies comparing phonics and whole language methods for teaching reading:

	Date	Size of Sample	Ages	Superior Method	Location
Brown (1998)	1997	120	7-9	Phonics	Texas
Cohen (1997)	1994	1,500	6-8	Phonics	California
Ebersoll (1999)	1988	800	5-6	Whole Language	Washington

✔ Guideline 8: If your topic reaches across disciplines, consider reviewing studies from each discipline separately.

Some topics naturally transcend discipline boundaries. For instance, if you were writing about diabetes management among teenage girls, you would find relevant sources in several discipline areas, including health care, nutrition, and psychology. The health care literature, for example, may deal with variations in insulin therapies (such as variations in types of insulin used or the use of pumps vs. syringes to deliver the insulin). The nutrition journals, on the other hand, may include studies on alternative methods for managing food intake in the search for more effective methods to control episodes of insulin shock. Finally, the psychological literature may offer insights into the nature of the stressors common to adolescent girls, especially with respect to how these stressors may interfere with the girls' decision-making processes concerning self-monitoring, nutrition choices, and value orientations. While these examples are hypothetical, it is easy to see how such a review might benefit from being divided into three sections, with the findings from each discipline area reviewed separately.

✔ Guideline 9: Write a conclusion for the end of the review.

The end of your literature review should provide closure for the reader, that is, the path of the argument should end with a conclusion of some kind. How you end a literature review, however, will depend on your reasons for writing it. If the review was written to stand alone, as in the case of a term paper or a review article for publication, the conclusion needs to make clear how the material in the body of the review has supported the assertion or proposition presented in the introduction.

On the other hand, a review in a thesis, dissertation, or journal article presenting original research usually leads to the research questions that will be addressed.

If your review is long and complex, you should briefly summarize the main threads of your argument, and then present your conclusion. Otherwise, you may cause your reader to pause in order to try to reconstruct the case you have made. Shorter reviews usually do not require a summary, but this judgment will depend on the complexity of the argument you have presented. You may need feedback from your faculty adviser or a friend to help you determine how much you will need to restate at the end. Example 8.9.1 presents only half of the two-paragraph summary of a very complex and comprehensive literature review. The author follows this with a series of detailed recommendations (a) for future research by scholars interested in family processes and family functioning and (b) for the application of these findings in the marriage and family counseling therapeutic setting.

Example 8.9.1[6]
Example of a summary for a complex review:

Given the growing ability of outsiders to unveil family secrets, the findings of this review may prove useful to researchers interested in the literature on controlling or withholding information in the family arena. A greater understanding of the family becomes possible through the study of secrets. Whereas some scholars defined secrecy in negative terms, others compared it to the more socially accepted concept of privacy. However, a more neutral view of secrecy allows the opportunity to broaden its scope. For instance, previously offered definitions did not allow researchers the opportunity to explore secrecy in a variety of contexts as the focus was only on that which was negatively valued. (p. 39)

✓ Guideline 10: Check the flow of your argument for coherence.

One of the most difficult skills to learn in academic writing is to evaluate one's own writing for coherence. Coherence refers to how well a manuscript holds together as a unified document. It is important for you to ask yourself how well the various elements of your review connect with one another. This requires that you carefully evaluate the effectiveness of the rhetorical elements of your document that tell the reader about its structure and about the relationships among its elements. Subheadings often go a long way in identifying a manuscript's structure. Transitional expressions and other kinds of rhetorical markers also help to identify relationships among sections, as in "the next example," "in a related study," "a counter-example," and "the most recent (or relevant) study." Obviously, there are many more such examples. Remember, these kinds of rhetorical devices are useful

---

[6] Brown-Smith, N. (1998). Family secrets. *Journal of Family Issues, 19*(1), 20-42.

navigational tools for your reader, especially if the details of the review are complex.

Activities for Chapter 8

1. Reread the three review articles in Supplementary Readings, and locate the paragraph(s) in which the authors describe what the contents of their reviews will be. How did the authors indicate what would be covered in their reviews?

2. Consider the subheadings in the three literature reviews.
- What function do the subheadings play in advancing the "argument" of the literature review?
- To what extent do the subheadings help the reader know what will and will not be covered in the reviews?

3. Locate three examples that illustrate the use of transitions. Were the transitions needed? Explain.

4. Locate the conclusions for the three reviews. Which one of the three presents the most straightforward summary of the contents of the review? What function do the other two summary statements play?

Notes

Chapter 9

Guidelines on Style, Mechanics, and Language Usage

The previous two chapters dealt with more general issues involved in writing a literature review. This chapter presents guidelines that are designed to focus on more specific issues related to style, mechanics, and language usage. These issues are important in producing an error-free draft.

✓ Guideline 1: Compare your draft with your topic outline.

The topic outline you prepared in Chapter 6 traced the path of the argument of your literature review. Now that your first draft is completed, you need to compare what you have written with the topic outline to make sure you have properly fleshed out the path of the argument.

✓ Guideline 2: Check the structure of your review for parallelism.

The reader of a literature review, especially a complex review, needs to be able to follow the structure of the manuscript while internalizing the details of the analysis and synthesis of the individual studies you have discussed. A topic outline will typically involve parallel structural elements—a discussion of weaknesses will be balanced by a discussion of strengths, arguments for a position will be balanced by arguments against, and so on. These expectations on the part of the reader stem from long-standing rhetorical traditions in academic writing. Therefore, you need to check your manuscript to make sure that your descriptions are balanced properly. This may require that you explain a particular lack of parallelism, perhaps by stating explicitly that no studies were found that contradict a specific point (see Guideline 8 in Chapter 7 if this applies to your review).

✓ Guideline 3: Avoid overusing direct quotations, especially long ones.

One of the most stubborn problems for novice academic writers in the social and behavioral sciences is the overuse of quotations. This is understandable, given the heavy emphasis placed in college writing classes on the correct use of the conventions for citing others' words. In fact, there is nothing inherently wrong about using direct quotations. However, problems arise when they are used inappropriately or indiscriminately.

A direct quotation presented out of context may not convey the full meaning of the original author's intent. When a reader struggles to understand the function of a quotation in a review, the communication of the message of the review is interrupted. Explaining the full context can further confuse the reader with details that are not essential for the purpose of the review in hand. By contrast, paraphrasing the main ideas of an author is more efficient, and it makes it easier to avoid extraneous details. In addition, paraphrasing eliminates the potential for disruptions in the flow of a review due to the different writing styles of various authors.

Of course, direct quotations are appropriate at times. For instance, you may want to use an excerpt that was written with a particular flair or that gives an emotional kick. Or, you may want to illustrate the original author's skill in writing or lack thereof. There may be other reasons for using direct quotations. However, they should be used sparingly, and long quotations should almost always be avoided altogether. Furthermore, quotations should not stand alone, isolated conceptually from the prose that immediately surrounds them. Example 9.3.1 illustrates an effective use of a direct quotation. Note that in this example, the writer emphasizes the poignancy of Akers' words in introducing the quotation, and then follows it up with an interpretation.

Example 9.3.1[1]

Unfortunately, as Ronald Akers poignantly pointed out (1996, p. 11), "in most public discourse about criminal justice policy, the underlying theoretical notions are ill-stated and vaguely understood. A policy may be adopted for political, economic, or bureaucratic reasons, then a theoretical rationale is formulated or adopted to justify the policy." As a consequence, a program may be driven by no single coherent theory but instead by an admixture of several or even conflicting theoretical positions. (p. 329)

Finally, it is seldom acceptable to begin a literature review with a quotation. Some students find it hard to resist doing this. Remember that it is usually very difficult for the reader to experience the intended emotional impact when the quotation is presented before the author has established the proper context.

✓ Guideline 4: Check your style manual for correct use of citations.

Make sure to check the style manual used in your field for the appropriate conventions for citing references in the text. For example, the *Publication Manual*

---

[1] Zhang, S. X. (1998). In search of hopeful glimpses: A critique of research strategies in current boot camp evaluations. *Crime & Delinquency, 44*, 314-334.

of the American Psychological Association style manual specifies the following guidelines for citations.[2]

    a. You may formally cite a reference in your narrative in one of several ways. At the conclusion of a statement that represents someone else's thoughts, you cite the author's last name and the year of publication, separated by a comma, set off in parentheses as in this example (Doe, 1999). If you use the author's name in the narrative, simply give the year of publication in parentheses immediately following the name, as in "Doe (1999) noted that..."

    b. When you cite multiple authors' names in parentheses, use the ampersand (&) instead of the word "and." If the citation is in the narrative, use the word "and."

    c. Use semicolons to separate multiple citations in parentheses, as in this example: (Black, 1999; Brown, 1998; Green, 2000).

    d. When you cite a secondary source, be sure you have made it clear, as in this example: (Doe, as cited in Smith, 1998). Note that only Smith (1998) would be placed in the reference list.

✔ Guideline 5: Avoid using synonyms for recurring words.

The focus of a review of empirical research should be on presenting, interpreting, and synthesizing other writers' ideas and research findings as clearly and precisely as possible. This may require you to repeat words that describe routine aspects of several studies. Students who are new to academic writing sometimes approach the task as though it were a creative writing exercise. *It is not!* Literature reviews should include numerous details about many studies, all of which the reader should be able to internalize quickly. Therefore, it is important to adhere to the use of conventional terms, even if they should recur. Clarity is best achieved when the writer consistently uses conventional terms throughout, especially when referring to details about a study's methodology or some other technical aspect of the research,

In general, it is best not to vary the use of labels. For example, if a study deals with two groups of participants, and the researcher has labeled them Groups 1 and 2, you should usually avoid substituting more creative phrases (e.g., "the Phoenix cohort" or "the original group of youngsters"). On the other hand, if alternative labels help clarify a study's design (e.g., when Group 1 is the control group and Group 2 the experimental group), use the substitute expressions instead, but remain consistent throughout your discussion. Example 9.5.1 illustrates how the use of synonyms and "creative" sentence construction can confuse readers. At various points, the first group is referred to as the "Phoenix cohort," as "Group I," and as the "experimental group," which is bound to cause confusion. Example

---

[2] American Psychological Association (1994). *Publication manual of the American Psychological Association*, 4th Ed. Washington, D.C.: American Psychological Association.

9.5.2 is an improved version in which the writer consistently uses the terms "experimental group" and "control group" to identify the two groups.

Example 9.5.1

The Phoenix cohort, which was taught to correctly identify the various toy animals by name, was brought back to be studied by the researchers twice, once after six months and again at the end of the year. The other group of youngsters was asked to answer the set of questions only once, after six months; but they had been taught to label the animals by color rather than by name. The performance of Group I was superior to the performance of Group II. The superior performance of the experimental group was attributed to...

Example 9.5.2

The experimental group was taught to identify toy animals by color and was retested twice at six-month intervals. The control group, which was taught to identify the toys by name, was retested only once after six months. The performance of the experimental group was superior to the performance of the control group. The superior performance of the control group was attributed to...

✔ Guideline 6:   Spell out all acronyms when you first use them, and avoid using too many.

So many acronyms become a part of the everyday lexicon that it is easy for them to be overlooked during the editing process. Some examples are school acronyms, like UCLA and USC; professional acronyms, like APA and MLA; and acronyms from our everyday lives, like FBI, TWA, and GPA. As obvious as this guideline may seem, it is quite common to find these and other examples of acronyms that are never spelled out. Make sure to check your document carefully for acronyms and spell them out the first time you use them.

Sometimes, it is useful to refer to something by its acronym, especially if its full title is long and you need to refer to it several times. For example, the Graduation Writing Assessment Requirement (GWAR) for students in the California State University is commonly referred to as the GWAR. In general, you should avoid using too many acronyms, especially ones that are not commonly recognized, like GWAR. In a complex literature review, using a few acronyms may be helpful, but using too many of them may be confusing.

✔ Guideline 7: Avoid the use of contractions; they are inappropriate in formal academic writing.

Contractions are a natural part of language use. They are one example of the natural process of linguistic simplification that accounts for how all languages change, slowly but surely, across time. Many instructors, even some English composition instructors, tolerate the use of contractions on the assumption that their use reflects the changing standards of acceptability in modern-day American English. In spite of such attitudes, however, it is almost always *inappropriate* to use contractions in formal academic writing.

✔ Guideline 8: When used, coined terms should be set off in quotations.

It is sometimes useful to coin a term to describe something in one or two words that would otherwise require a sentence or more. Coined terms frequently become part of common usage, as in the noun "lunch," which is now commonly used as a verb (Did you *lunch* with Jane yesterday?). However, coined terms should be used sparingly in formal academic writing. When you feel you should coin a term, set it off with quotation marks to indicate that its meaning cannot be found in a standard dictionary.

✔ Guideline 9: Avoid slang expressions, colloquialisms, and idioms.

Remember that academic writing is *formal* writing. Therefore, slang, colloquialisms, and idioms are not appropriate in a literature review. While many slang terms such as "cool" (meaning "good") and "ain't" are becoming part of our conversational language repertoires, in formal writing they should be avoided altogether. Colloquialisms, such as "thing" and "stuff" should be replaced by appropriate noncolloquial terms (e.g., "item," "feature," and "characteristic"). Similarly, idioms, such as "to rise to the pinnacle" and "to survive the test" should be replaced by more formal expressions, such as "to become prominent" and "to succeed" or "to be successful."

✔ Guideline 10: Use Latin abbreviations in parenthetic material; elsewhere, use English translations.

The Latin abbreviations shown below, with their English translations, are commonly used in formal academic writing. With the exception of et al., these abbreviations are limited to parenthetic material. For instance, the Latin abbreviation in parentheses at the end of this sentence is proper: (i.e., this is a correct example). If this was not in parentheses, you should use the English translation, that is, this is also a correct example. Also, note the punctuation that is required for each of these abbreviations.

cf.	compare	etc.	and so forth
e.g.,	for example	i.e.,	that is
et al.	and others	vs.	versus, against

✔ Guideline 11: Check your draft for common writing conventions.

There are a number of additional writing conventions that all academic disciplines require. Check your draft to ensure you have applied all these rules before you give it to your instructor to read.

a. Make sure you have used complete sentences.

b. It is sometimes acceptable to write a literature review in the first person. However, you should avoid excessive use of the first person.

c. It is inappropriate to use sexist language in academic writing. For instance, it is incorrect to always use masculine or feminine pronouns (he, him, his vs. she, her, hers) to refer to a person when you are not sure of the person's gender (as in, "the teacher left her classroom...," when the teacher's sex is not known). Often, sexist language can be avoided by using the plural form ("the teachers left their classrooms..."). If you must use singular forms, alternate between masculine and feminine forms.

d. You should strive for clarity in your writing. Thus, you should avoid indirect sentence constructions, such as "In Smith's study, it was found...." An improved version would be, "Smith found that ...."

e. In general, numbers from zero through nine are spelled out, but numbers 10 and above are written as numbers. Two exceptions to this rule are numbers assigned to a table or figure and measurements expressed in decimals or in metrical units.

f. Always capitalize nouns followed by numerals or letters when they denote a specific place in a numbered series. For instance, this is Item f under Guideline 11 in Chapter 9.

g. Always spell out a number when it is the first word or phrase in a sentence, as in, "Seventy-five participants were interviewed...."

✔ Guideline 12: Write a concise and descriptive title for the review.

The title of a literature review should identify the field of study you have investigated as well as tell the reader your point of view. However, it should also be concise and descriptive of what you have written. In general, the title should not draw attention to itself; rather, it should help the reader to adopt a proper frame of reference with which to read your paper. The following suggestions will help you to avoid some common problems with titles.

a. **Identify the field, but do not describe it fully.** Especially with long and complex reviews, it is not advisable for you to try to describe every aspect of your argument. If you do, the result will be an excessively long and detailed title. Your title should provide your reader an easy entry into your paper. It should not force the reader to pause in order to decipher it.

b. **Specify your bias, if you have one.** If your review is written with an identifiable bias, it is important to specify your point of view in the title. For instance, if you are critical of some aspect of the literature, consider using a phrase such as "A Critique of..." or "A Critical Evaluation of..." as part of your title.

c. **Avoid "cute" titles.** Avoid the use of puns, alliteration, or other literary devices that call attention to the title. While a title such as "Phonics vs. 'Hole' Language" may seem clever if your review is critical of the Whole Language approach to reading instruction, it will probably distract the reader. A more descriptive title, such as "Reading as a Natural or Unnatural Outgrowth of Spoken Language," will give the reader a better start in comprehending your paper.

d. **Keep it short.** Titles should be short and to the point. Professional conference organizers will often limit titles of submissions to about nine words in order to facilitate the printing of hundreds of titles in their program books. While such printing constraints are not at play with a term paper or a chapter heading, it is still advisable to try to keep your review title as simple and short as possible. A good rule of thumb is to aim for a title of about 10 words, plus or minus two.

✔ Guideline 13: Strive for a user-friendly draft.

You should view your first draft as a work in progress. As such, it should be formatted in a way that invites comments from your readers. Thus, it should be legible and laid out in a way that allows the reader to react to your ideas easily. The following list contains some suggestions for ensuring that your draft is user-friendly. Ask your faculty adviser to review this list and add additional items as appropriate.

a. **Spell-check, proofread and edit your manuscript.** New word processing programs have spell-check functions. Use the spell-check feature before asking anyone to read your paper. However, there is no substitute for editing your own manuscript carefully, especially since the spell-check function can overlook your mistakes (e.g., "see" and "sea" are both correctly spelled, but the spell-check function will not highlight them as errors if you mistakenly type the wrong one). Remember that your goal should be to have an error-free document that communicates the content easily and does not distract the reader with careless mechanical errors.

a. **Number all pages.** Professors sometimes write general comments in the form of a memo in addition to their notes in the margins. Unnumbered pages make such comments more difficult to write because professors cannot refer to page numbers in their memos.

b. **Double-space the draft.** Single-spaced documents make it difficult for the reader to write specific comments or suggest alternative phrasing.

c. **Use wide margins.** Narrow margins may save paper, but they restrict the amount of space available for your instructor's comments.

d. **Use a stapler or a strong binder clip to secure the draft.** Your draft is one of many papers your instructor will read. Securing the document with a stapler or a strong clip will make it easier to keep your paper together. If you use a folder or a binder to hold your draft, make sure that it opens flat. Plastic folders that do not open flat make it difficult for the reader to write comments in the margins.

e. **Identify yourself as the author, and include a telephone number or e-mail address.** Because your draft is one of many papers your instructor will read, it is important to identify yourself as the author. Always include a cover page with your name and a telephone number or e-mail address in case your professor wants to contact you. If you are writing the literature review as a term paper, be sure to indicate the course number and title as well as the date.

f. **Make sure the draft is printed clearly.** In general, you should avoid using printers with ribbons unless you make sure the print is dark enough for it to be read comfortably. Similarly, if you submit a photocopy of your draft, make sure the copy is dark enough. Always keep a hard copy for your records! Student papers sometimes get misplaced, and hard drives on computers sometimes crash.

g. **Avoid "cute" touches.** In general, you should avoid using color text for highlighted words (use italics instead), mixing different size fonts (use a uniform font size throughout), and using clip-art or any other special touches that may distract the reader by calling attention to the format of your paper instead of its content.

✔ Guideline 14: Avoid plagiarism at all costs.

If you are uncertain about what constitutes plagiarism, consult your university's student code of conduct. It is usually part of your university's main catalog and is reprinted in several other sources readily available to students. For example, the University of Washington's Psychology Writing Center makes available a handout on Plagiarism and Student Writing on its Website (access from the university's main Web page: <http://www.washington.edu>). This handout is linked to a statement on academic responsibility prepared by the University's Committee on Academic Conduct (1994)[3], that lists six kinds of plagiarism.

(1) Using another writer's words without proper citation;

(2) Using another writer's ideas without proper citation;

(3) Citing a source but reproducing the exact words of a printed source without quotation marks;

(4) Borrowing the structure of another author's phrases or sentences without crediting the author from whom it came;

(5) Borrowing all or part of another student's paper or using someone else's outline to write your own paper; and

(6) Using a paper-writing service or having a friend write the paper for you. (p. 23)

It is easy to quarrel about whether borrowing even one or two words would constitute plagiarism or whether an "idea" is really owned by an author. However, plagiarism is easily avoided simply by making sure that you cite your sources properly. If you have any doubt about this issue with respect to your own writing, ask your instructor. This is a very serious matter.

✔ Guideline 15: Get help if you need it.

It should be obvious from the content of this chapter that the expectations for correctness and accuracy in academic writing are quite high. If you feel that you are unable to meet these demands at your current level of writing proficiency, you may need to get help. International students are often advised to hire proofreaders to help them meet their instructors' expectations. Most universities offer writing classes, either through the English department or in other disciplines. Some offer workshops for students struggling with the demands of thesis or dissertation requirements, and many universities have Writing Centers that provide a variety of services for students. If you feel you need help, talk with your instructor about the services available at your university. You should not expect your instructor to edit your work for style and mechanics.

Activities for Chapter 9

1. Compare the titles of the three review articles in Supplementary Readings.
    *   How well does each title serve to identify the field of the review?

---

[3] Committee on Academic Conduct. (1994). *Bachelor's degree handbook*, University of Washington.

- Do these titles specify what the authors' point of view in the review will be?

2. Now consider your own first draft of your literature review.
   - Compare your first draft with the topic outline you prepared. Do they match? If not, where did your draft vary from the outline? Does this variation affect the path of the "argument" of your review?
   - Find two or three places in your review where your discussion jumps to the next major category of your topic outline. How will the reader know that you have changed to a new category (i.e., did you use subheadings or transitions to signal the switch)?

Chapter 10

Incorporating Feedback and Refining the First Draft

At this point in the writing process, you have completed the major portion of your critical review of the literature. However, your work is not yet done. You should now undertake the important final steps in the writing process—redrafting your review.

New writers often experience frustration at this stage because they are now expected to take an impartial view of a piece of writing in which they have had a very personal role. In the earlier stages, as the writer, you were the one who was analyzing, evaluating, and synthesizing other writers' work. Now, your draft is the subject of your own and your readers' analysis and evaluation. This is not an easy task, but it is a critical and necessary next step in writing an *effective* literature review.

The first step in accomplishing this role reversal is to put the manuscript aside for a period of time, thereby creating some distance from the manuscript and from your role as the writer. Second, remind yourself that the writing process is an ongoing negotiation between a writer and the intended audience. This is why the role reversal is so important. You should now approach your draft from the perspective of someone who is trying to read and understand the argument that is being communicated.

The redrafting process typically involves evaluating and incorporating feedback. That feedback may come from an instructor and your peers, or it may come from your own attempts to refine and revise your own draft. If you are writing a literature review as a term paper, you should solicit feedback from your professor at key points during the writing process, either by discussing your ideas during an office visit or, if your professor is willing, by submitting a first draft for comments. If it is for a thesis or dissertation, your earliest feedback will be from your faculty adviser, although you should also consider asking fellow students and colleagues for comments. If the review is for an article intended for publication, you should seek feedback from instructors, fellow students, and colleagues.

As the writer, you should determine which comments you will incorporate and which you will discard, but the feedback you receive from these various sources will give you valuable information on how to improve the communication of your ideas to your audience. The following guidelines are designed to help you through this process.

✔ Guideline 1: The reader is always right.

This guideline is the most important in the redrafting process. If the reader has not understood one of your points, the communication process has not worked. Therefore, you should change the draft to make it clearer for the reader. To put it simply, the reader is always right. It will not help you to waste your time by trying to defend the draft manuscript. Instead, try to determine why the reader did not understand it. Did you err in your analysis? Did you provide insufficient background information? Would the addition of more explicit transitions between sections make it clearer? These, and questions like these, should guide your discussions with your readers.

✔ Guideline 2: Expect your instructor to comment on the content.

It is important for you to obtain your instructor's feedback on the *content* of your manuscript early in the redrafting process. If your first draft contained many stylistic and mechanical errors, such as misspellings or misplaced headings, your instructor may feel compelled to focus on these matters and defer the comments on the content until the manuscript is easier to read. If this occurs, be prepared to ask your instructor for additional feedback on your paper's content. Furthermore, even if your instructor returns your draft with few marks and comments, you should not assume that silence about your paper's content means that there is no room for improvement. You should ask your instructor specific questions about your paper to generate the kind of feedback you need in order to properly revise your manuscript. Did you cover the literature adequately? Are your conclusions about the topic justified? Are there gaps in your review? How can the paper be improved? You need, and are entitled to, answers to questions such as these at this stage in the process.

✔ Guideline 3: Concentrate first on comments about your ideas.

As the previous guideline suggests, your first priority at this stage should be to make sure that your ideas have come across as you intended them. Of course, you should note comments about stylistic matters and eventually attend to them, but your first order of business should be to ensure that you have communicated the argument you have developed. Thus, you need to evaluate carefully the feedback you receive from all your sources—your fellow students as well as your instructor—because at this stage you need to concentrate your efforts on making sure that your paper communicates your ideas effectively and correctly.

✔ Guideline 4: Reconcile contradictory feedback by seeking clarification.

Inevitably, you will encounter differences of opinion among those who review your draft document. For instance, it is not unusual for members of a thesis or dissertation committee to give you contradictory feedback. One member may ask that you provide additional details about a study while another member may want you to de-emphasize it. If you encounter such differences of opinion, it is your responsibility to seek further clarification from both sources and to negotiate a resolution of the controversy. First, you need to make sure that the different opinions were not due to one person's failure to comprehend your argument. Second, you need to discuss the matter with both individuals and arrive at a compromise solution.

✔ Guideline 5: Reconcile comments about style with your style manual.

Make sure that you have carefully reviewed the particular style manual that is required for your specific writing task. If your earliest experience with academic writing was in an English department course, you may have been trained to use the style manual of the Modern Language Association.[1] Many university libraries advise that theses and dissertations follow the University of Chicago style manual.[2] However, the most widely used manual in the social and behavioral sciences is the style manual of the American Psychological Association.[3] If you are preparing a paper for publication, check the specific periodical or publisher for guidelines on style before submitting the paper. Finally, many academic departments and schools will have their own policies with respect to style. Regardless of which style manual pertains to your writing task, remember that you are expected to adhere to it meticulously. As you consider incorporating any feedback you receive, make sure that it is in conformity with the required style manual.

✔ Guideline 6: Allow plenty of time for the feedback and redrafting process.

Students often experience frustration when they are faced with major structural or content revisions and are up against a deadline. You can expect to have to prepare at least one major redraft of your literature review, so you should allow yourself plenty of time for it. Professional writers often go through five or more drafts before they consider a document to be a final draft. While you may not have quite so many drafts, you should allow enough time to comfortably go through at least several revisions of your document.

---

[1] Gibaldi, J. (1990). *MLA style manual and guide to scholarly publishing. 2nd Ed.* New York: Modern Language Association of America.

[2] University of Chicago Press (1993). *The Chicago manual of style. 14th Ed.* Chicago: University of Chicago Press.

[3] American Psychological Association (1994). *Publication manual of the American Psychological Association. 4th Ed.* Washington, D.C.: American Psychological Association.

Activities for Chapter 10

1. Ask two friends to read the draft of your literature review and to comment on the content. Compare the comments from your two friends.
- On which points did your friends agree?
- On which points did they disagree? Which of the two opinions will you follow? Why?
- Consider the places in your review that your friends found hard to follow. Rewrite these passages, keeping in mind that you want your friends to understand your points.

2. Write five questions designed to guide your instructor or your friends in giving you feedback on the content of your review.
- Reread your review draft and respond to your own questions by pretending you are your instructor.
- Revise your draft according to your own feedback.
- Reconsider the five questions you wrote for your instructor. Which questions would you leave on your list? What questions would you add?

Chapter 11

Comprehensive Self-editing Checklist for Refining the Final Draft

As has been emphasized frequently in this book, your final draft should be as accurate and error-free as possible, both in terms of its content as well as its mechanics and style. After you have carefully considered the feedback you received from your peers and academic advisers and after you have revised the manuscript in light of their input, you should carefully edit your manuscript a final time. The purpose for this final review is accuracy.

The following checklist is grouped according to some of the major criteria instructors use in evaluating student writing. Most of these criteria are absolutely critical when writing a thesis or dissertation. However, your instructor may relax some of them in the case of term papers written during a single semester.

You will find that most of the items on the checklist were presented in the earlier chapters as guidelines, but many additional ones have been added in an attempt to cover common problems that are sometimes overlooked by student writers. You should show this checklist to your instructors and ask that they add or eliminate items according to their own preferences.

Keep in mind that the checklist is designed to help you to refine the manuscript. Ultimately, the extent of perfection you achieve will depend on how meticulously you edit your own work.

Adherence to the Writing Process for Editing and Redrafting

_____ 1. Have you asked your instructors to review this checklist and to add or delete items according to their preferences?

_____ 2. After finishing your last draft, did you set your manuscript aside for several days before you began to revise it (i.e., did you create an appropriate _distance_ from your manuscript before changing roles from "writer" to "reader")?

_____ 3. Did you ask another person to review your manuscript?

_____ 4. Have you addressed all of the questions raised by your reviewers?

_____ 5. Did you reconcile all differences of opinion among your reviewers?

Importance or Significance of the Topic

_____ 6. Is your topic important, either from a theoretical or a practical perspective?

_____ 7. Does it present a fresh perspective or identify a gap in the literature (i.e, does it address a question not previously addressed)?

_____ 8. Is your topic's significance or importance demonstrated and justified?

_____ 9. Is this an appropriate topic for your field of study?

_____ 10. Is the topic timely in terms of what is being reported in the research literature?

_____ 11. Does the title of your manuscript adequately describe the subject of your review?

Organization and Other Global Considerations

_____ 12. Does your review include an introduction and a discussion and conclusions section?

_____ 13. Did you include a reference list?

_____ 14. Does the length and organization of your review follow the criteria set forth by (a) your instructor, if you are writing a term paper; (b) your committee chair, if you are writing a thesis or dissertation; or (c) the publication guidelines of the journal you have targeted, if you are writing for publication?

Effectiveness of the Introduction

_____ 15. Does your introduction describe the scope of the literature you have reviewed and why the topic is important?

_____ 16. Did you describe in your introduction the general structure of your paper?

_____ 17. Does your introduction identify the line of argumentation you have followed in your manuscript?

_____ 18. Does the introduction state what will and will not be covered, if this is appropriate?

_____ 19. Does the introduction specify your thesis statement or point of view, if this is relevant?

Currency and Relevance of the Literature Cited

_____ 20. Did you review the most current articles on the topic?

_____ 21. Are the studies you reviewed current?

_____ 22. If you have included older articles, did you have a good reason for including them?

_____ 23. Have you explained why you have described some findings as being strong?

_____ 24. Have you explained why you have described other findings as being weak?

_____ 25. Did you identify the major patterns or trends in the literature?

_____ 26. Have you identified in your manuscript the classic or landmark studies you cited?

_____ 27. Did you specify the relationship of these classic studies to subsequent studies they may have influenced?

Thoroughness and Accuracy of the Literature Reviewed

_____ 28. Is the coverage of your review adequate?

_____ 29. Have you noted and explained the gaps _in the literature_?

_____ 30. Have you described any pertinent controversies in the field?

_____ 31. If you answered yes to item 30, did you make clear which studies fall on either side of the controversy?

_____ 32. Have you checked the draft for parallelism?

_____ 33. Have you noted and explained the relationships among studies, such as which ones came first? Which ones share similarities? Which ones have differences?

_____ 34. Did you indicate the source of key terms or concepts?

_____ 35. Are there gaps _in the body of your manuscript_?

Coherence and Flow of the Path of the Argument

_____ 36. Does each study you reviewed correspond with a specific part of your topic outline?

_____ 37. Have you deleted citations to studies you decided not to include in your review because they do not relate to the path of your argument?

_____ 38. Is the path of your argument made clear throughout the manuscript?

_____ 39. Does each part of your review flow logically from the preceding part?

_____ 40. If you have used "meta-comments" (see Chapter 8, Guideline 6), are they essential?

_____ 41. If you have used subheadings, do they help to advance your argument?

_____ 42. If you have not used subheadings, would adding them help advance your argument?

_____ 43. Is your manuscript coherent, or would additional transitional devices help to clarify how it holds together?

Effectiveness of the Conclusion

_____ 44. Does your conclusion provide closure for the reader?

_____ 45. Does your conclusion make reference to the line of argumentation you specified in the introduction?

Accuracy of Citations and the Reference List

_____ 46. Have you checked your style manual's guidelines for citing references in the narrative (e.g., when to use parentheses, how to cite multiple authors, and how to cite a secondary source)?

_____ 47. Have you checked each citation in the manuscript to make sure that it appears on your reference list?

_____ 48. Have you checked all entries on the reference list to make sure that each one is cited in your manuscript?

_____ 49. Have you eliminated all entries from your reference list that are not cited in the manuscript?

_____ 50. Have you checked for accuracy and consistency between the dates in your manuscript and the dates in your reference list?

_____ 51. Have you checked for accuracy between the spelling of the authors' names in your manuscript and in your reference list?

_____ 52. Are most of the dates of the studies included in the reference list within the recent past?

Mechanics and Overall Accuracy of the Manuscript

_____ 53. Did you read and edit your manuscript carefully?

_____ 54. Did you perform a final spell-check of the entire manuscript?

_____ 55. Are your margins set appropriately?

_____ 56. Did you number all the pages?

_____ 57. Is your manuscript double-spaced?

_____ 58. Did you include your full name (and, for theses and dissertations, your telephone number)?

Appropriateness of Style and Language Usage

_____ 59. Have you carefully reviewed the appropriate style manual for your field?

_____ 60. Have you checked your manuscript for consistency with your style manual?

_____ 61. Are your headings formatted in accordance with the guidelines specified in the appropriate style manual?

_____ 62. If you used Latin abbreviations (i.e., e.g., etc.), are they in parentheses, and have you checked for the required punctuation?

_____ 63. If you have used long quotations, are they absolutely necessary?

_____ 64. Does each quotation contribute significantly to the review?

_____ 65. Can any of these quotations be paraphrased?

_____ 66. Did you avoid the use of synonyms for important key terms and concepts?

_____ 67. If you have coined a new term, did you set it off in quotations?

_____ 68. Have you avoided slang terms and colloquialisms?

_____ 69. Have you avoided using contractions?

_____ 70. Have you included any annotations that are not linked to the path of the argument of your review?

_____ 71. Have you avoided using a series of annotations?

_____ 72. Have you spelled out all acronyms on first mention?

_____ 73. If you have used the first person, was it appropriate?

_____ 74. Have you avoided using sexist language?

_____ 75. If you used numbers in the narrative of your review, have you checked to see if you spelled out the numbers zero through nine?

_____ 76. If you used a noun followed by a number to denote a specific place in a sequence, did you capitalize the noun (as in Item 76 of the checklist)?

_____ 77. If you used a number to begin a sentence, did you spell it out?

Grammatical Accuracy

_____ 78. Did you check your manuscript for grammatical correctness?

_____ 79. Is every sentence of your manuscript a complete sentence?

_____ 80. Have you avoided using indirect sentence constructions (as in, "In Galvan's study, it was found….")?

_____ 81. Have you been consistent in your use of tenses (e.g., if you use the present tense in describing one study's findings, did you use this same tense throughout, unless you were commenting on the historical relationship among studies)?

_____ 82. Have you checked for the proper use of commas and other punctuation marks?

_____ 83. Have you attempted to avoid using complicated sentence structures?

_____ 84. If you have any long sentences (e.g., several lines), have you attempted to break them down into two or more sentences?

_____ 85. If you have any long paragraphs (e.g., a page or longer), have you attempted to break them down into two or more paragraphs?

Additional Editing Steps for Non-native English Speakers and Students with Serious Writing Difficulties

_____ 86. If your proficiency in English is not at a high level, have you asked a proofreader for assistance?

_____ 87. Have you checked the entire manuscript for proper article (e.g., a, an, the) usage?

_____ 88. Have you checked the manuscript for proper use of prepositions?

_____ 89. Have you checked each sentence for proper subject-verb agreement?

_____ 90. Have you checked the manuscript for the proper use of idiomatic expressions?

Guidelines Suggested by Your Instructor

_____ 91.

_____ 92.

_____ 93.

_____ 94.

_____ 95.

Supplementary Readings

Sample Literature Reviews for
Discussion and Evaluation

Notes

Review A

Individual Differences in Student Cheating[1]

There can be little doubt that cheating occurs in college students. There is a long history of studies on the frequency of cheating in the United States (see Davis, Grover, Becker, & McGregor, 1992, for a review), and this research has recently been extended into the United Kingdom (Franklyn-Stokes & Newstead, 1995). No precise figures can be given as to incidence because this depends on how cheating is defined and how it is measured. However, the American research has repeatedly shown that more than half of university students indulge in some form of cheating behavior during their undergraduate years and the British studies suggest that the figure is not markedly different in the United Kingdom. Although such figures are surprising and perhaps disturbing, from a psychological perspective the more interesting questions surround the factors that influence cheating behavior and the reasons why some students cheat more than others.

The research literature on cheating has tended to be largely descriptive, so that we now know much about the incidence and correlates of cheating and much less about the reasons for the observed differences. A possible conceptual framework can be provided by considering two factors that seem inherently likely to be implicated in explaining cheating behavior: motivation and morality. The contribution of each of these will be considered in turn.

With respect to motivation, there is evidence that those with high achievement motivation are more likely to cheat than those with lower levels. Type A behavior (Friedman & Rosenman, 1959), which involves high striving for achievement, has been found to correlate posi-

tively with both observed and reported cheating (Perry, Kane, Bernesser, & Spicker, 1990; Weiss, Gilbert, Giordano, & Davis, 1993). However, the full picture is almost certainly more complicated than this because it seems likely that only some forms of achievement motivation might lead to cheating. Dweck (1986) has drawn the distinction between students with performance goals (those who wish simply to achieve good grades in their courses) and students with learning goals (those who wish to learn from their studies). Related, though not identical, distinctions have been made by Ames (1984) between ability and mastery goals and by Nicholls (1984) between ego involvement and task involvement. Individuals with learning goals are more likely to persist in challenging tasks and may even seek them out, and it is reasonable to suggest that such students will be less likely to resort to cheating as a way of coping with a challenging situation. There is little direct evidence on this issue, though Weiss et al. found that those who studied to learn (as measured by Eison's, 1981, scale) rather than to obtain a good grade were less likely to cheat.

Turning now to morality, once again the direct evidence is sparse but there is an indication that moral development is related to cheating. It has been found that scores on moral reasoning tests correlate negatively with the occurrence of cheating (Grimm, Kohlberg, & White, 1968; Malinowski & Smith, 1985). Note, however, that cheating in these studies involved cheating on experimental tasks, not on assessments. Other research has indicated that students who cheat in the classroom tend to "neutralize" (rationalize) their behavior, blaming it on the situation rather

[1] Literature review excerpt from: Newstead, S. E., Franklyn-Stokes, A., & Armstead, P. (1996). Individual differences in student cheating, *Journal of Educational Psychology, 88*, 229-241. The excerpt appears on pages 229-231. Copyright © 1996 by the American Psychological Association, Inc. All rights reserved. Reprinted with permission.

than on themselves (e.g., Haines, Diekhoff, La-Beff, & Clark, 1986). Neutralization involves denial of responsibility, condemnation of condemners, and appeal to higher authorities; all these are ways of protecting the individual from blame and hence from moral disapproval. Neutralization, however, is likely to be a consequence rather than a cause of cheating.

While the literature relating cheating to both motivation and morality is not voluminous, these two concepts provide a useful perspective from which to view the existing research on cheating. Most of this research is descriptive and focuses on group differences in the incidence of cheating. These differences, which have included dimensions such as gender, age, academic achievement, and discipline studied, are reviewed and, where appropriate, related to the concepts of motivation and morality.

Gender

There is considerable evidence in the literature that females report less cheating than males. This was found to be consistently the case by Davis et al. (1992) in their survey of more than 6,000 students and has also been reported by many other researchers, including Baird (1980) and Calabrese and Cochran (1990). There are, however, a number of exceptions to this finding. Haines et al. (1986) and Houston (1983) found no differences between the sexes. Jacobson, Berger, and Millham (1970) even found that females cheated significantly more often than males.

Gender differences in motivation may help explain these findings since it has been found that female university students tend to be more intrinsically motivated than male students (Vallerand et al., 1992). Intrinsically motivated students are studying for the pleasure and satisfaction of doing so and hence seem unlikely to cheat. Gender differences might also be related to differences in moral reasoning, though the evidence that females have a better developed sense of moral responsibility is controversial (see, for example, Thoma, 1986). There is some evidence that females admit to as much cheating as males when this is of an altruistic nature, that is, is done to help another student (Calabrese & Cochran, 1990).

Age

Previous research has suggested that university students are less likely to cheat than those in high school (Davis et al., 1992). Some studies have found that students in the later years of their degree course are less likely to cheat than those in their early years (e.g., Bowers, 1964; Baird, 1980), though other studies have found little difference in relation to year of study (Stern & Havlicek, 1986). These differences between students of differing experience may be attributable to the fact that the more experienced students were slightly older; alternatively, they may be related to the different cultures and opportunities present in the different years of study, or to the fact that some of the weaker students, who may be more likely to cheat, have been weeded out during the early years of their course.

There is relatively little research that has looked directly at the effects of age, although this is a dimension that is becoming increasingly important in higher education as the proportion of mature and nontraditional students increases. Haines et al. (1986) found that there was a negative correlation between age of student and reported incidence of cheating; indeed, this variable was the most powerful of the many predictors of cheating that they studied in their research. Franklyn-Stokes and Newstead (1995) found in their first study that students aged 25 years or older were perceived by other students and lecturers to cheat less often than those aged either 21-24 or 18-20 years. Their second study found that both the older age group and the youngest students reported cheating less than the 21-24 year olds. This is clearly an area in which further data are required.

Motivational differences seem a plausible candidate for explaining the effects of age. There is considerable evidence that older students may be studying for more intrinsic, personal rewards than those who go straight to university from school (see Richardson, 1994, for a recent review). Explanations of age differences in terms of moral development cannot be ruled out, because there is considerable evidence for age-related development in moral reasoning, even over the short period of a degree course (Murk & Adelman, 1992; Rest & Thoma, 1985), though this may be due to the influences of education rather than age itself.

Academic Achievement

In general, it seems that more successful students are less likely to cheat. This conclusion emerges from studies that have correlated grade point average (GPA) with observed and reported incidence of cheating. Hetherington and Feldman (1964) found that student cheating in experimentally contrived situations was higher for students with low GPAs. Similarly, Bowers (1964) and Haines et al. (1986) found that GPA correlated negatively with the extent to which students reported cheating.

The achievement of high grades is, not surprisingly, related to motivation (see, for example, Pintrich & Garcia, 1991). However, it is possible that high achievers also have a better developed sense of moral responsibility and hence explanations in terms of both motivation and morality are possible.

Discipline Studied

A wide variety of disciplines have been studied in previous research, but it is not easy to compare such studies because they have typically used tailor-made questionnaires; therefore, direct comparisons of the frequencies of cheating are invalid. Relatively few studies have systematically compared the incidence of cheating in different disciplines. The most important study to date of interdisciplinary differences was carried out some years ago in the United States by Bowers (1964). In a national survey involving over 5,000 students in 11 different majors, he found that certain disciplines were associated with more cheating than others: Business and engineering were associated with the highest rates of cheating; education, social science, and science were in the middle; and arts and humanities had the lowest rates. It is not easy to relate these differences to either motivation or to morality. It is possible that business and engineering students tend to have performance goals whereas arts and humanities students have learning goals, but there is little direct evidence on this.

It is clear from the existing research that there are many issues requiring further clarification and elaboration. In the present research we investigated differences in cheating as a function of gender, age, academic achievement, and discipline studied. In addition, we used a measure of the extent to which students adopted high academic standards and asked students to indicate their reasons for studying for a degree; both of these were intended to obtain insights into students' motivation.

The present research involved the use of a questionnaire designed to elicit self-reported frequency of 21 different cheating behaviors. In addition to indicating whether they had indulged in cheating, respondents were also asked to give their reasons for cheating or not cheating. Reasons for not cheating seem not to have been studied before, despite their potential theoretical and practical implications. There are, however, a number of studies that have investigated reasons for cheating and that provide indications as to what to expect. The received wisdom is that the major factors are time pressure and the competition to get good grades (e.g., Barnett & Dalton, 1981). Reasons for cheating are of particular interest because of the potential light they can shed on theories of cheating behavior: They provide information both on students' motivation and on their morality.

We designed Study 1 to investigate the incidence of a number of different cheating behaviors. This enabled us to relate this incidence to gender, age, academic achievement, academic standards, and discipline studied. By examining the reasons given for cheating and not cheating, we hoped to shed some light on the underlying causes of cheating and to relate these to current theories of motivation and moral development.

Notes

Review B

Knowledge, Interest, and Narrative Writing[1]

In 1932, Hemingway wrote that "A good writer should know as near everything as possible" (p. 191). In the past decade, psychologists and educators have rediscovered that to know more is to write better (e.g., DeGroff, 1987; Kellogg, 1987; Langer, 1984; McCutchen, 1986; Voss, Vesonder, & Spilich, 1980). More recently, psychologists also have considered the role that interest plays in writing (e.g., Hidi & Anderson, 1992; Hidi & McLaren, 1991), although very few empirical investigations have been conducted in the area (Hidi & McLaren, 1990).

Several questions remain unanswered about the roles that knowledge and interest play in effective writing. For example, do writers' knowledge of and interest in a topic explain a significant proportion of variance in writing measures beyond that explained by students' knowledge of discourse structure? Does interest explain a significant amount of variance beyond that explained by topic knowledge? Furthermore, do knowledge and interest interact in their effects on writing? Finally, do knowledge and interest interact with gender and grade level in influencing writing? Such questions led us to investigate narrative writing.

Specifically, we examined (a) whether discourse knowledge, topic knowledge, and individual interest interact in their relationship with writing and (b) whether grade level and gender interact with topic knowledge and interest. In addition, we investigated whether topic knowledge and individual interest are related to the interestingness of writers' narrative texts. Finally, we sought empirical evidence that topic knowledge and individual interest actually measure different constructs. We begin by describing briefly the Flower and Hayes (1981) writing model, which provided the theoretical foundation for our study.

Flower and Hayes (1981) Model

Flower and Hayes (1981) proposed a model of writing processes that they derived from protocol analyses of writers as the writers composed aloud. The model has three main components: the task environment, the writer's long-term memory, and the writing processes. Elements in the task environment include the writing topic, the intended audience, motivating factors, and elements of text already produced (e.g., notes, outlines, or drafts) that provide external storage of ideas. The long-term memory component includes knowledge of the topic, audience, and types of writing plans (expository, narrative, etc.). Together, the task environment and the long-term memory influence the interactive and iterative writing processes of planning, translating, and reviewing.

Planning involves three subprocesses: generating, organizing, and goal setting. Writers generate ideas by accessing relevant information about the writing topic from long-term memory and from the task environment. Writers organize ideas by imposing a meaningful structure that fits well with readers' expectations. In goal setting, writers plan how to convey their ideas in a meaningful way to the intended audience. In translating, writers transform ideas into written

---

text, which requires knowledge of vocabulary and of rules of standard written language. Reviewing is a continual process that involves the writer's evaluation and revision of text according to internal standards and perceived audience expectations.

In this study, we limited our investigation to indicants of the planning and translating processes. Writers thus wrote only one draft of a narrative passage without having the opportunity to revise. We expected that, along with interest, two elements of long-term memory would be related to indicants of writing processes: discourse knowledge and topic knowledge.

Discourse Knowledge

Discourse knowledge concerns what one knows about how to write. More specifically, discourse knowledge "consists of schemata for various discourse forms, procedures and strategies involved in instantiation of those schemata, and local sentence-generation procedures (including grammatical knowledge)" (McCutchen, 1986, p. 432). Such knowledge is important to writers for writing grammatically correct prose, for generating sentences that are cohesively linked, and for writing coherently. Older students presumably have more and better organized knowledge about text structure (McCutchen, 1986). In fact, writers become competent with discourse knowledge rather late in their development of literacy (Chomsky, 1965).

Discourse knowledge is important for rapid processing of verbal information. For example, Hunt and colleagues (Hunt, 1978; Hunt, Frost, & Lunneborg, 1973; Hunt, Lunneborg, & Lewis, 1975) compared high- and low-discourse knowledge college students on tasks requiring encoding, attending, rehearsing, chunking, searching long-term memory, and holding and manipulating information in long-term memory. Students with high discourse knowledge processed information more accurately and rapidly than did low-discourse knowledge students. Benton and colleagues (Benton & Kiewra, 1986; Benton, Kraft, Glover, & Plake, 1984) found similar results on tasks requiring writers to unscramble scrambled letters, words, sentences, and paragraphs. In both high school and undergraduate

samples, skilled writers performed these tasks faster and more accurately than did less skilled writers. In addition, college students' performance on the tasks was positively related to their discourse knowledge.

These findings support Kellogg's (1987) view that the relationship between discourse knowledge and writing ability may have the most to do with the translating process. Translating requires transforming ideas (semantics) into written symbols that satisfy the constraints of standard rules of the language (e.g., syntax). Discourse knowledge makes writing (i.e., translating) automatic. Writers who have easier access to knowledge of discourse (e.g., grammar, punctuation, sentence structure, and text structure) translate their ideas more rapidly and accurately and, consequently, they produce more syntactically correct prose. Therefore, measures of discourse knowledge should be correlated with indicants of the translating process.

Topic Knowledge

How much writers know about a topic influences how well they write (e.g., DeGroff, 1987; Kellogg, 1987; Langer, 1984; McCutchen, 1986; Voss, et al., 1980). Langer (1984) believes this is the case because

> Intuition and experience suggest that when students write to a topic about which they have a great deal of well-integrated knowledge, their writing is more likely to be well organized and fluent; conversely, when students know little about a topic, their writing is more likely to fail. (Langer, 1984, p. 28)

McCutchen (1986) and Voss et al. (1980) examined how topic knowledge influences narrative writing with respect to descriptions of setting and actions. McCutchen and Voss et al. argued that a person with a great deal of topic knowledge would, in addition to describing the setting of a story, generate a meaningful sequence of actions and provide detail. However, someone with little knowledge of the topic would most likely be able to describe the setting but be unable to generate a sequence of actions that is both meaningful and detailed. In fact, Voss et al. found that undergraduates who had more knowledge about baseball generated a greater proportion of baseball game-related actions than did those with less baseball knowledge. Conversely, undergraduates with less baseball knowledge wrote stories that contained a greater proportion of topic-irrelevant information. Similarly, McCutchen (1986) found that elementary and middle school students who had a great deal of football knowledge wrote expository and narrative texts that contained a greater proportion of game-related actions than did the texts of football novices. In addition, high-football knowledge students wrote more coherent and lengthier texts than did low-football knowledge students. DeGroff (1987) found similar results with fourth-grade students who wrote on the topic of baseball.

Topic knowledge can enhance low-ability students' performance on topic-related tasks (e.g., Recht & Leslie, 1988; Schneider, Körkel, and Weinert, 1989; Walker, 1987). For example, Walker compared the recall performance of adults with high and low aptitudes (as defined by the U. S. Army aptitude test of general or technical ability) who were also identified as either baseball experts or baseball novices. Adults with low aptitudes who were baseball experts recalled more information from a baseball passage than did the adults with high aptitudes who were baseball novices. Similarly, Recht and Leslie (1988) and Schneider et al. (1989) found that children who had greater knowledge about a topic recalled more information from a passage about that topic than did children who had less knowledge. However, Recht and Leslie and Schneider et al. found neither a main effect for aptitude nor an interaction of Aptitude × Knowledge on children's text recall and comprehension of a baseball passage. These studies suggest that differences in topic knowledge may be more important than differences in aptitude and that individuals with low aptitudes may be able to perform effectively in a domain for which they have a great deal of knowledge (Schneider et al., 1989).

Differences in topic knowledge also can reverse expected age-related differences in cognitive performance (Schneider et al., 1989). Perhaps the best known study is that by Chi (1978), who compared child chess experts with adult chess novices. Chi found that although children performed worse on traditional memory-span tasks, the children outperformed the adults on

reproduction of chess positions that conformed to the rules of chess. Similarly, Körkel (1987) found that third-grade soccer experts recalled more text units from a soccer passage than did both fifth-grade and seventh-grade soccer novices. Together, these studies indicate that topic knowledge can enable a child expert to perform like an older expert and even better than an older novice.

Why is topic knowledge so important for the writing process? In proposing his workload hypothesis, Kellogg (1987) stated that "the more an individual knows about a topic, the less effortful it might be to retrieve and use the relevant knowledge in preparing a written document" (p. 258). The person with high knowledge has more information in memory on which to draw and takes less time than the person with low knowledge to retrieve it. For the person with high knowledge, the ideas come so rapidly that writing becomes automatic, to the point where the pen or keyboard can hardly keep up with the generating process. Consequently, the planning process is highly automated. The writer with high knowledge has more workload space to devote to setting goals and organizing ideas. Therefore, we expected the amount of topic knowledge to be related to indicants of the generating and organizing subprocesses of planning.

Interest

Educational psychologists have long asserted that interest directs attention and enhances learning (Dewey, 1913; James, 1890; Thorndike, 1935). Psychologists have recently begun to consider the role that interest plays in writing (e.g., Hidi, 1990; Hidi & Anderson, 1992; Hidi & McLaren, 1991). Some have suggested that interest influences students' writing because it combines what students know about a topic with what they value (Hidi & McLaren, 1991; Renninger, 1992). Therefore, some authors recommend that teachers have young children select their own writing topics (Gradwohl & Schumacher, 1989; Graves, 1975).

Most researchers believe that interest emerges from an individual's interaction with his or her environment (Krapp, Hidi, & Renninger, 1992). There are two distinct types of interest: (a) *individual* interest, which emerges from one's history of interaction with an object or a stimulus and (b) *situational* interest, which pertains to the specific characteristics of an event or object that capture one's interest (Hidi, 1990). Whereas individual interest is considered more of a psychological trait, situational interest is, by definition, more state specific. Our intent in the present study was to investigate the relationship between narrative writing and individual interest. Individual interest is thought to increase attention, concentration, effort, willingness to learn, and acquisition of knowledge (Renninger, 1992). On average, individual interest has been found to correlate about .30 with measures of academic achievement. Correlations tend to be stronger among male students than among female students and among older than among younger students (Schiefele, Krapp, & Winteler, 1992).

In their review of the literature, Hidi and McLaren (1990) did not find any empirical investigations of how individual interest is related to writing performance. In a follow-up study, Hidi and McLaren (1991) found that fourth and sixth graders did not write longer or qualitatively better expositions on topics that the students identified as being interesting than they did on those they identified as being uninteresting. Hidi and McLaren (1991) also found that although students are motivated to write on topics they find interesting, lack of topic knowledge may actually hinder their writing performance. On the other hand, students' writing may be enhanced if they have high knowledge about topics that they find relatively uninteresting.

On the basis of these findings, we expected that an interaction might be observed between topic knowledge and interest in terms of effects on indicants of planning (i.e., generating and organizing ideas) processes. Specifically, we hypothesized that high knowledge and low interest would be associated with lengthier and better organized writing than would low knowledge and low interest. In addition, high knowledge and high interest should have stronger effects than low knowledge and high interest.

Previous findings pertaining to gender and grade level differences (Schiefele et al., 1992) led us to predict that these variables also might interact with interest in their relationship to planning. In the present study, we chose the

writing topic of baseball. We therefore expected male students would know more about the writing topic. Consequently, we hypothesized that male students would outperform female students at low interest levels but that female students would perform comparably to male students at high interest levels. Furthermore, whereas older writers should outperform younger writers at low interest levels, younger writers should perform comparably to older writers at high interest levels.

Purpose and Predictions

Our purpose in the present study was to investigate whether discourse knowledge, topic knowledge, and individual interest are related to different measures of narrative writing performance. We were further interested in whether topic knowledge and interest interact with discourse knowledge, gender, or grade level in their relationships with writing. Our predictions were that (a) discourse knowledge should be related to indicants of the translating process; (b) topic knowledge should be related to indicants of the planning process (i.e., generating and organizing); (c) whereas male students with low interest should write lengthier and better organized stories than female students with low interest, female students with high interest should perform comparably to male students with high interest; (d) older students should be more successful than younger students at translating ideas into correct syntactic structure; (e) a developmental reversal may be observed on indicants of the planning process for younger students with high knowledge versus older students with low knowledge; and (f) whereas older writers with low interest should outperform younger writers with low interest, high interest should enable younger writers to perform comparably to older writers.

Review C

Immune Neglect: A Source of Durability Bias in Affective Forecasting[1]

I am the happiest man alive. I have that in me that can convert poverty into riches, adversity into prosperity, and I am more invulnerable than Achilles; fortune hath not one place to hit me.

–Sir Thomas Browne, *Religio Medici*

Imagine that one morning your telephone rings and you find yourself speaking with the king of Sweden, who informs you in surprisingly good English that you have been selected as this year's recipient of a Nobel prize. How would you feel, and how long would you feel that way? Although some things are better than instant celebrity and a significant bank deposit, most people would be hard pressed to name three, and thus most people would probably expect this news to create a sharp and lasting upturn in their emotional lives. Now imagine that the telephone call is from your college president, who regrets to inform you (in surprisingly good English) that the Board of Regents has dissolved your department, revoked your appointment, and stored your books in little cardboard boxes in the hallway. How would you feel, and how long would you feel that way? Losing one's livelihood has all of the hallmarks of a major catastrophe, and most people would probably expect this news to have an enduring negative impact on their emotional lives.

Such expectations are often important and often wrong. They are important because people's actions are based, in large measure, on their implicit and explicit predictions of the emotional consequences of future events. A decision to marry or divorce, to become a lawyer rather than a coronet player, or to pass up the twinkie at the convenience store in favor of a croissant from the inconvenient bakery is ordinarily predicated on the belief that one of these events will bring greater emotional rewards than the other. Indeed, affective forecasts are among the guiding stars by which people chart their life courses and steer themselves into the future (Baron, 1992; Herrnstein, 1990; Kahneman & Snell, 1990; Loewenstein & Frederick, 1997; Totterdell, Parkinson, Briner, & Reynolds, 1997). But are these forecasts correct? In some ways they undoubtedly are. For example, most people recognize that a weekend in Paris would be more enjoyable than gallbladder surgery, and few people fear chocolate or tingle in anticipation of next year's telephone directory. But even if people can estimate with some accuracy the *valence* and *intensity* of the affect that future events will evoke, they may be less adept at estimating the *duration* of that affect, and it is often the prediction of duration that shapes an individual's decisions. For instance, most people realize that divorce is anguishing and marriage is joyous, but the decision to commit oneself to either course is predicated not merely on one's beliefs about the valence and intensity of these emotional responses but also on one's beliefs about how long each response is likely to last. People invest in monogamous relationships, stick to sensible diets, pay for vaccinations, raise children, invest in stocks, and eschew narcotics because they recognize that maximizing their happiness requires that they consider not only how an event will make them feel at first but, more important, how long those feelings can be

[1] Literature review excerpt from: Gilbert, D. T., Pinel, E. C., Wilson, T. D., Blumberg, S. J., & Wheatley, T. P. (1998). Immune neglect: A source of durability bias in affective forecasting. *Journal of Personality and Social Psychology, 75*, 617-638. The excerpt appears on pages 617-620. Copyright © 1998 by the American Psychological Association, Inc. All rights reserved. Reprinted with permission.

expected to endure (see Ainslie, 1992; Mischel, Cantor, & Feldman, 1996).

The Durability Bias

How long *can* feelings be expected to endure? Although the telephone calls from Sweden and the administration building would leave most professors respectively delirious or disconsolate, research suggests that regardless of which call they received, their general level of happiness would return to baseline in relatively short order. Common events typically influence people's subjective well-being for little more than a few months (Suh, Diener, & Fujita, 1996; Wortman & Silver, 1989), and even uncommon events—such as losing a child in a car accident, being diagnosed with cancer, becoming paralyzed, or being sent to a concentration camp—seem to have less impact on long-term happiness than one might naively expect (e.g., Affleck & Tennen, 1996; Brickman, Coates, & Janoff-Bulman, 1978; Collins, Taylor, & Skokan, 1990; Diener, 1994; Helmreich, 1992; Kahana, Kahona, Harel, & Rosner, 1988; Lehman et al., 1993; Suedfeld, 1997; Taylor, 1983; Taylor & Armor, 1996; Wortman & Silver, 1987). The causes of the remarkable stability of subjective well-being are not fully understood (McCrae & Costa, 1994), but the consequences seem clear: Most people are reasonably happy most of the time, and most events do little to change that for long.

If these findings are surprising, it is only because they violate the intuition that powerful events must have enduring emotional consequences. We believe that such intuitions are profoundly mistaken and that people often tend to overestimate the duration of their affective responses to future events. There are at least six distinct reasons why such a *durability bias* might arise in affective forecasting. We briefly describe five of them and then concentrate on the sixth.

Misconstrual

It is understandably difficult to forecast one's reactions to events that one has never experienced because it is difficult to know precisely what those events will entail. Although most people feel certain that they would not enjoy going blind, phrases such as "going blind" actually describe a wide range of events (e.g., slowly losing one's eyesight as a result of a congenital defect or suddenly losing one's eyesight during a heroic attempt to rescue a child from a burning house), and these events may have an equally wide range of emotional consequences. Research suggests that when people think about an event, they often fail to consider the possibility that their particular, momentary conceptualization of the event is only one of many ways in which they might have conceptualized it and that the event they are imagining may thus be quite different from the event that actually comes to pass (Dunning, Griffin, Milojkovic, & Ross, 1990; Griffin, Dunning, & Ross, 1990; Griffin & Ross, 1991). When forecasters misconstrue an event and imagine it as more powerful than it actually turns out to be, they will naturally overestimate the duration of their affective responses.

Inaccurate Theories

It may be difficult to forecast one's affective reactions to events about which one knows little, but it can be just as difficult to forecast one's affective reactions to events about which one knows a lot. Both culture and experience provide people with detailed, domain-specific knowledge about how particular events are likely to make them feel ("A bris is a happy occasion as long as it isn't mine"), and some of that knowledge is bound to be wrong. For instance, Ross (1989) has shown that North Americans vastly overestimate the strength and frequency of the emotional distress that women experience before menstruation. One might expect that experience with such ordinary events would cure misconceptions about them, but the ability to remember one's emotional experiences accurately is so prone to error and distortion that inaccurate theories about the affective consequences of ordinary events may persist indefinitely (Fredrickson & Kahneman, 1993; Mitchell & Thompson, 1994). Because some of one's acquired wisdom about the emotional consequences of common events is undoubtedly wrong ("Getting rich is the key to permanent happiness"), the affective forecasts that this wisdom generates ("If I win the lottery, I'll live happily ever after") will undoubtedly be wrong too.

Motivated Distortions

Affective forecasts do more than merely guide people into the future. They also comfort, inspire, and frighten people in the present (Elster & Loewenstein, 1992). So, for example, people may overestimate the duration of their affective responses to the positive events they anticipate ("After Joel and I get married, life will be wonderful") because the mere act of making that forecast induces positive affect ("Just thinking about the wedding makes me smile!"). Similarly, people may overestimate the duration of their negative affective responses as a form of "defensive pessimism" that braces them against the consequences of a negative event and thus leaves them pleasantly surprised when those consequences turn out to be less enduring than they had predicted (Norem & Cantor, 1986; Rachman, 1994). People may even use dire affective forecasts to motivate themselves to expend effort in the pursuit of desirable ends (Mischel et al., 1996). For example, just as parents often exaggerate the negative consequences of certain behaviors to control their children's actions ("If you let go of my hand in the store and get lost, why don't we just plan to meet over by the Child Eating Monster?"), people may exaggerate the negative affective consequences of certain outcomes to motivate themselves to pursue one course of action over another ("If I flunk the algebra test tomorrow, I will be doomed to a life of poverty, disease, and despair. So I'd better skip the party and hit the library"). In short, affective forecasts have immediate affective consequences, and thus it is only natural that they should sometimes be made in service of their immediate effects. The durability bias may be the result of that service.

Undercorrection

When people attempt to predict the duration of their affective responses ("How would I feel a week after getting fired?"), they may first imagine their initial affective response ("As soon as I saw the pink slip I'd crawl under my desk and weep") and then correct for the passage of time ("But I guess I'd get up eventually, go home, and make popcorn"; Gilbert, Gill, & Wilson, 1998). Experiments in a variety of domains indicate that when judgments are made in this fashion, they tend to suffer from undercorrection (Gilbert, 1991; Tversky & Kahneman, 1974), and people seem especially susceptible to this problem when correcting their predictions for the passage of time (Kahneman & Snell, 1992; Prelec & Loewenstein, 1997; Read & Loewenstein, 1995). Because affective reactions are generally most intense at the onset, the tendency to undercorrect a prediction of one's initial reaction will typically produce a durability bias.

Focalism

When people attempt to predict their affective reactions to a particular event, they naturally focus on that event to the exclusion of others. So, for example, when a mother is asked to imagine how she would feel 7 years after the death of her youngest child, she is likely to focus exclusively on that tragedy and fail to consider the many other events that will inevitably unfold over that time period, capture her attention, require her participation, and hence influence her general affective state. Indeed, it would be truly perverse for a mother to pause and consider how much this sort of heartache might be assuaged by her other child's portrayal of the dancing banana in the school play, an important new project at work, or the taste of an especially gooey caramel on a cloudless summer day. But the fact of the matter is that trauma does not take place in a vacuum: Life goes on, and nonfocal events do happen and do have affective consequences. As such, perverse or not, accurate affective forecasts must somehow take those consequences into account. Because nonfocal events are likely to absorb attention and thus neutralize affective responses to focal events (Erber & Tesser, 1992), the failure to consider them should generally cause people to overestimate the duration of their affective responses (Wilson, Wheatley, Meyers, Gilbert, & Axsom, 1998).

All five of the foregoing mechanisms may cause the durability bias, all five are important, and all five require careful empirical analysis (see Gilbert & Wilson, in press). Nonetheless, in this article we concentrate on a sixth cause of the durability bias.

Immune Neglect

In the quotation that opened this article, Sir Thomas Browne claimed to have something inside him that could convert adversity into prosperity, thus allowing him to claim the title of happiest man alive. Whatever that thing was, most ordinary people seem to have it too. In science, literature, and folklore, people are famous for making the best of bad situations, remembering their successes and overlooking their excesses, trumpeting their triumphs and excusing their mistakes, milking their glories and rationalizing their failures—all of which allows them to remain relatively pleased with themselves despite all good evidence to the contrary. Psychologists from Freud to Festinger have described the artful methods by which the human mind ignores, augments, transforms, and rearranges information in its unending battle against the affective consequences of negative events (e.g., Festinger, 1957; Freud, 1936; Greenwald, 1980; Kunda, 1990; Steele, 1988; Taylor, 1983, 1991; Taylor & Armor, 1996; Taylor & Brown, 1988). Some of these methods are quite simple (e.g., dismissing as a rule all remarks that begin with "You drooling imbecile"), and some are more complicated (e.g., finding four good reasons why one didn't really want to win the lottery in the first place); taken in sum, however, they seem to constitute a psychological immune system that serves to protect the individual from an overdose of gloom. As Vaillant (1993, p. 11) noted: "Defense mechanisms are for the mind what the immune system is for the body." Ego defense, rationalization, dissonance reduction, motivated reasoning, positive illusions, self-serving attribution, self-deception, self-enhancement, self-affirmation, and self-justification are just some of the terms that psychologists have used to describe the various strategies, mechanisms, tactics, and maneuvers of the psychological immune system.

One of the hallmarks of the psychological immune system is that it seems to work best when no one is watching, and when its operations are explicitly scrutinized, it may cease functioning altogether. People may convince themselves that they never really loved the ex-spouse who left them for another, but when a friend reminds them of the 47 love sonnets that

they conveniently failed to remember writing, the jig is up, the fix is spoiled, and they shuffle off sheepishly to nurse old wounds (and find new friends). The mental machinery that transforms adversity into prosperity must work quietly if it is to work at all, and successful rationalization typically requires that rationalizers not regard themselves as such (Gur & Sackheim, 1979). People, then, may be generally unaware of the influence that their psychological immune system has on their emotional well-being (Loewenstein & Adler, 1995; Snell, Gibbs, & Varey, 1995), and it is easy to imagine how this tendency—which we call *immune neglect*—might give rise to the durability bias. If people fail to recognize that their negative affect will not merely subside but will be actively antagonized by powerful psychological mechanisms that are specifically dedicated to its amelioration, then they will naturally tend to overestimate the longevity of those emotional reactions (see Loewenstein & Frederick, 1997).

Of the six mechanisms that can cause the durability bias, immune neglect is unique in an important way. Although five of these mechanisms—misconstrual, inaccurate theories, motivated distortion, and focalism—may lead people to overestimate the duration of both their positive and negative affective reactions, immune neglect should lead people to overestimate the duration of their negative affective reactions only. As Taylor (1991, p. 67) observed, "Once the threat of the negative event has subsided, counteracting processes are initiated that reverse, minimize, or undo the responses elicited at the initial stage of responding," and "this pattern seems to distinguish negative events from positive or neutral ones." Indeed, evidence suggests that although people do actively work to neutralize or transform their negative affect ("Phil was never really right for me, and I was able to see that much more clearly the moment he took back the engagement ring"), they generally do not actively work to augment their positive affect because active psychological work has the paradoxical consequence of neutralizing positive affect (Erber & Tesser, 1992; Erber, Wegner, & Therriault, 1996; Isen, 1987; Parrott, 1993; cf. Wegener & Petty, 1994). In short, the immune system works to repair one, not to improve one, and this suggests that immune ne-

glect should cause a negative—but not a positive—durability bias.

Appendix A
A Closer Look at Locating Literature Electronically*

Increasingly, students are being given direct access to electronic databases in academic libraries. In this topic, we will consider how to use them to locate articles in academic journals.

We will explore some of the important principles for locating literature electronically (via computer) from three major sources: (1) *Sociofile,* which contains the print versions of *Sociological Abstracts* and *Social Planning Policy & Development Abstracts,* covering journal articles published in over 1,600 journals; (2) PsycLIT, which contains the print version of *Psychological Abstracts,* with abstracts to journal articles worldwide since 1974;[1] and (3) *ERIC,* which contains abstracts to articles in education found in more than 600 journals from 1966 to date.[2] The following characteristics are true of all three databases.

First, for each journal article, there is a single *record;* a record contains all the information about a given article. Within each record, there are separate *fields* such as the title field, the author field, the abstract (that is, summary of the article) field, and the descriptor field.

A descriptor is a key subject-matter term; for example, *learning environments, learning disabilities,* and *learning theories* are descriptors in *ERIC.* One of the important ways to access the databases is to search for articles using appropriate descriptors. To determine which descriptors are available, each database has a *thesaurus.* It is important to refer to it to identify the terms you want to use in your search. For example, if your topic is *group therapy for child molesters,* the appropriate descriptors in PsycLIT are *group psychotherapy and pedophilia.*

The following are some principles for conducting a search. First, we can search a particular field or search entire records. If you have identified appropriate descriptors in the *thesaurus,* it is usually sufficient to search the descriptors fields using the descriptors.[3]

We may conduct a search for all articles containing either (or both) of two descriptors by using OR. For example, the instruction to find "dyslexia" OR "learning disabilities" will locate all articles with either one of these descriptors. Thus, using OR broadens our search.

We can also broaden our search by using a root word such as *alcohol* followed by an asterisk (*); the asterisk instructs the program to search for the plural form as well as derivatives such as *alcoholism* and *alcoholics.*

Frequently, we wish to narrow our search in order to make it more precise. An important instruction for doing this is *AND.* For instance, if we use the instruction to locate articles with *"learning environments AND dyslexia,"* the program will only identify articles with *both* these descriptors, and exclude articles that have only one of them.

We can also make our search more precise by using NOT. The instruction *"advertising NOT television"* will identify all articles relating to advertising but exclude any that relate to advertising on television.

If you are working in a field with thousands of references, you can be more precise by adding another search concept such as age group (child, adolescent, adult, or elderly) and population (human or animal).

If you are required to use only recent references, you can also limit the search to recent years.

Reprinted with permission from Patten, M.L. (1997). *Understanding Research Methods: An Overview of the Essentials.* Los Angeles: Pyrczak Publishing. Copyright © 1997 by Pyrczak Publishing. All rights reserved.

[1]Use the print version for journal articles published before 1974.

[2]The emphasis in this topic is on journal articles. Note that PsycLIT also abstracts books, *Sociofile* also abstracts dissertations, and *ERIC* also abstracts unpublished documents such as convention papers, which are available on microfiche.

[3]If you are not able to find appropriate descriptors, conduct a "free text" search, using your own terms (such as *child molester,* which is not a *thesaurus* term) and searching entire records. If this term appears in any field in any of the records, the record(s) will be selected. If any are selected, examine the descriptors field to see what descriptors have been assigned to it—noticing *pedophilia,* you could now search again looking only in the descriptors field for the *thesaurus* descriptor, *pedophilia.*

Appendix B
Sample ERIC Search

Descriptors: Child Language, Language Acquisition, and/or Cognitive Development

1. Gestures, Signs, and Words in Early Language Development. **Author**: Capirci, Olga; Volterra, Virginia; Montanari, Sandro **Source**: New Directions for Child Development **Year**: 1998

2. The Development of Gesture and Speech as an Integrated System. **Author**: Goldin-Meadow, Susan **Source**: New Directions for Child Development **Year**: 1998

3. Word Learning in a Special Population: Do Individuals with Williams Syndrome Obey Lexical Constraints. **Author**: Stevens, Tassos; Karmiloff-Smith, Annette **Source**: Journal of Child Language **Year**: 1997

4. Autonomous Linguistic Systems in the Language of Young Children. **Author**: Levy, Yonata **Source**: Journal of Child Language **Year**: 1997

5. Linguistic Cues in the Acquisition of Number Words. **Author**: Bloom, Paul; Wynn, Karen **Source**: Journal of Child Language **Year**: 1997

6. The Puzzle of Negation: How Children Move from Communicative to Grammatical Negation in ASL. **Author**: Anderson, Diane E.; Reilly, Judy S. **Source**: Applied Psycholinguistics **Year**: 1997

7. Language Awareness and the Autonomous Language Learner. **Author**: Little, David **Source**: Language Awareness **Year**: 1997

8. Categorization and Its Developmental Relation to Early Language. **Author**: Gershkoff-Stowe, Lisa; Thal, Donna J.; Smith, Linda B.; Namy, Laura L. **Source**: Child Development **Year**: 1997

9. Music and Language Development in Early Childhood: Integrating Past Research in the Two Domains. **Author**: Chen-Hafteck, Lily **Source**: Early Child Development and Care **Year**: 1997

10. Hitting a Moving Target: Acquisition of Sound Change in Progress by Philadelphia Children. **Author**: Roberts, Julie **Source**: Language Variation and Change **Year**: 1997

11. Differential Productivity in Young Children's Use of Nouns and Verbs. **Author**: Tomasello, Michael; Akhtar, Nameera; Dodsen, Kelly; Rekau, Laura **Source**: Journal of Child Language **Year**: 1997

12. Acquisition of Variable Rules: A Study of (-t, d) Deletion in Preschool Children. **Author**: Roberts, Julie **Source**: Journal of Child Language **Year**: 1997

13. The Acquisition of Personal Pronouns in French-Speaking and English-Speaking Children. **Author**: Girouard, Pascale C.; Ricard, Marcelle; Decarie, Therese Gouin **Source**: Journal of Child Language **Year**: 1997

14. Children's Individual Approaches to the Organization of Narrative. **Author**: Wigglesworth, Gillian **Source**: Journal of Child Language **Year**: 1997

15. Determiner Phrases and the Debate on Functional Categories in Early Child Language. **Author**: Bohnacker, Ute **Source**: Language Acquisition **Year**: 1997

16. Binding Conditions in Young Children's Grammar: Interpretation of Pronouns Inside Conjoined NPs. **Author**: Matsuoka, Kazumi **Source**: Language Acquisition **Year**: 1997

17. Slot and Frame Patterns and the Development of the Determiner Category. **Author**: Pine, Julian M.; Lieven, Elena V. M. **Source**: Applied Psycholinguistics **Year**: 1997

18. Bugs and Birds: Children's Acquisition of Second Language Vocabulary through Interaction. **Author**: Ellis, Rod; Heimback, Rick **Source**: System **Year**: 1997

19. Lexically Based Learning and Early Grammatical Development. **Author**: Lieven, Elena V. M. **Source**: Journal of Child Language **Year**: 1997

20. The Differential Effect of Storybook Reading on Preschoolers' Acquisition of Expressive and Receptive Vocabulary. **Author**: Senechal, Monique **Source**: Journal of Child Language **Year**: 1997

21. Children's Acquisition of Speech Timing in English: A Comparative Study of Voice Onset Time and Final Syllable Vowel Lengthening. **Author**: Snow, David **Source**: Journal of Child Language **Year**: 1997

22. The Structure of Age: In Search of Barriers to Second Language Acquisition. **Author**: Bialystok, Ellen **Source**: Second Language Research **Year**: 1997

23. Early Parent-Child Interaction Grammar Prior to Language Acquisition. **Author**: Duncan, Starkey, Jr. **Source**: Language & Communication **Year**: 1996

24. The Structure and Acquisition of Relative Clauses in Serbo-Croatian. **Author**: Goodluck, Helen; Stojanovic, Danijela **Source**: Language Acquisition **Year**: 1996

25. Phonological Acquisition and Dutch Word Prosody. **Author**: Lohuis-Weber, Heleen; Zonneveld, Wim **Source**: Language Acquisition **Year**: 1996

26. The Development of Pragmatic Competence: Past Findings and Future Directions for Research. **Author**: Thompson, Linda **Source**: Current Issues in Language and Society **Year**: 1996

27. Knowledge and Acquisition of the Spanish Verbal Paradigm in Five Communities. **Author**: Schnitzer, Marc L. **Source**: Hispania **Year**: 1996

28. The Acquisition of Prosodic Structure: An Investigation of Current Accounts of Children's Prosodic Development. **Author**: Kehoe, Margaret; Stoel-Gammon, Carol **Source**: Language **Year**: 1997

29. Conversations with Vovo: A Case Study of Child Second Language Acquisition and Loss. **Author**: Coughlan, Peter J. **Source**: Issues in Applied Linguistics **Year**: 1995

30. Young Children's Acquisition of the Handshape Aspect of American Sign Language Signs: Parental Report Findings. **Author**: Siedlecki, Theodore, Jr.; Bonvillian, John D. **Source**: Applied Psycholinguistics **Year**: 1997

31. Beginning to Read in Turkish: A Phonologically Transparent Orthography. **Author**: Oney, Banu; Durgunoglu, Aydin Yucesan **Source**: Applied Psycholinguistics **Year**: 1997

32. Children, Adolescents, and Language Change. **Author**: Kerswill, Paul **Source**: Language Variation and Change **Year**: 1996

33. Learning from a Connectionist Model of the Acquisition of the English Past Tense. **Author**: Plunkett, Kim; Marchman, Virginia A. **Source**: Cognition **Year**: 1996

34. "Talking": Beginnings Workshop. **Author**: Palmer, Wolf Dennie; And Others **Source**: Child Care Information Exchange **Year**: 1996

35. Knowledge of Binding in Normal and SLI Children. **Author**: Franks, Steven L.; Connell, Phil J. **Source**: Journal of Child Language **Year**: 1996

36. Categorization and Feature Specification in Phonological Acquisition. **Author**: Gierut, Judith A. **Source**: Journal of Child Language **Year**: 1996

37. Syntactic Categories in the Speech of Young Children: The Case of the Determiner. **Author**: Pine, Julian M. Martindale, Helen **Source**: Journal of Child Language **Year**: 1996

38. Ties Between Lexical and Grammatical Development: Evidence from Early-Talkers. **Author**: Thal, Donna J.; And Others **Source**: Journal of Child Language **Year**: 1996

39. Pointing and Social Awareness: Declaring and Requesting in the Second Year. **Author**: Franco, Fabia; Butterworth, George **Source**: Journal of Child Language **Year**: 1996

40. Why Do Infants Begin to Talk? Language as an Unintended Consequence. **Author**: Locke, John L. **Source**: Journal of Child Language **Year**: 1996

41. Young Two-Year-Olds' Tendency to Map Novel Verbs onto Novel Actions. **Author**: Merriman, William E.; And Others **Source**: Journal of Experimental Child Psychology **Year**: 1996

42. Perception of Motherese in a Signed Language by 6-Month-Old Deaf Infants. **Author**: Masataka, Nobuo **Source**: Development Psychology **Year**: 1996

43. Quantification without Qualification. **Author**: Crain, Stephen; And Others **Source**: Language Acquisition **Year**: 1996

44. The Acquisition of Relative Clauses: Movement or No Movement? **Author**: Labelle, Marie **Source**: Language Acquisition **Year**: 1996

45. Nativism Does Not Equal Universal Grammar. **Author**: Wolfe-Quintero, Kate **Source**: Second Language Research **Year**: 1996

46. The Case of Total Deafness II: Phrasing in the Prelinguistic Vocalizations of a Child with Congenital Absence of Cochleas. **Author**: Lynch, Michael P. **Source**: Applied Psycholinguistics **Year**: 1996

47. Analyzing Language Sequence in the Sequence of Language Acquisition. **Author**: Ellis, Nick C. **Source**: Studies in Second Language Acquisition **Year**: 1996

48. Grammatical Knowledge and Memorized Chunks. A Response to Ellis. **Author**: Ioup, Georgette **Source**: Studies in Second Language Acquisition **Year**: 1996

49. Using Time-Series Research Designs to Investigate the Effects of Instruction on SLA. **Author**: Mellow, J. Dean; And Others **Source**: Studies in Second Language Acquisition **Year**: 1996

50. Insights to Language from the Study of Gesture: A Review of Research on the Gestural Communication of Non-signing Deaf People. **Author**: Morford, Jill P. **Source**: Language & Communication **Year**: 1996

51. The Association between Language and Symbolic Play at Two Years: Evidence from Deaf Toddlers. **Author**: Spencer, Patricia Elizabeth **Source**: Child Development **Year**: 1996

52. Gradual Development of L2 Phrase Structure. **Author**: Vainikka, Anne; Young-Scholten, Martha **Source**: Second Language Research **Year**: 1996

53. Collocations and Cultural Connotations of Common Words. **Author**: Stubbs, Michael **Source**: Linguistics and Education **Year**: 1995

54. The Implications of "First Language Acquisition As a Guide for Theories of Learning and Pedagogy" in a Pluralistic World. **Author**: Meehan, Teresa M.; And Others **Source**: Linguistics and Education **Year**: 1995

55. Early Syntactic Acquisition in German: Evidence for the Modal Hypothesis. **Author**: Ingram, David; Thompson, William **Source**: Language **Year**: 1996

56. Book Reviews. "Beyond Names for Things: Young Children's Acquisition of Verbs." **Author**: Schwanenflugel, Paula J.; Noyes, Caroline R. **Source**: Merrill-Palmer Quarterly **Year**: 1996

57. Developmental Issues in Interlanguage Pragmatics. **Author**: Kasper, Gabriele; Schmidt, Richard **Source**: Studies in Second Language Acquisition **Year**: 1996

58. Interactions Between the Acquisition of French Object Drop and the Development of the C-System. **Author**: Muller, Natascha **Source**: Language Acquisition **Year**: 1996

59. Functional Categories in Child L2 Acquisition of French. **Author**: Grondin, Nathalie; White, Lydia **Source**: Language Acquisition **Year**: 1996

60. The Early Stages in Adult L2 Syntax: Additional Evidence from Romance Speakers. **Author**: Vainikka, Anne; Young-Scholten, Martha **Source**: Second Language Research **Year**: 1996

61. Is Language Created or Manufactured? **Author**: Stokoe, William C. **Source**: Sign Language Studies **Year**: 1995

62. A Crossdisciplinary Perspective on Studies of Rapid Word Mapping in Psycholinguistics and Behavior Analysis. **Author**: Wilkinson, Krista M.; And Others **Source**: Developmental Review **Year**: 1996

63. Colour Term Knowledge in Two-Year-Olds: Evidence for Early Competence. **Author**: Shatz, Marilyn; And Others **Source**: Journal of Child Language **Year**: 1996

64. Eighteen-Month-Old Children Learn Words in Non-ostensive Contexts. **Author**: Tomasello, Michael; And Others **Source**: Journal of Child Language **Year**: 1996

65. Early Passive Acquisition in Iniktitut. **Author**: Allen, Shanley E. M.; Crago, Martha B. **Source**: Journal of Child Language **Year**: 1996

66. An Experimental Test of Phonemic Cyclicity. **Author**: Gierut, Judith A. **Source**: Journal of Child Language **Year**: 1996

67. Context-Sensitive Underspecification and the Acquisition of Phonemic Contrasts. **Author**: Dinnsen, Daniel A. **Source**: Journal of Child Language **Year**: 1996

68. Consonant Clusters in Child Phonology and the Directionality of Syllable Structure Assignment. **Author**: Lleo, Conxita; Prinz, Michael **Source**: Journal of Child Language **Year**: 1996

69. Infants' Sensitivity to Word Boundaries in Fluent Speech. **Author**: Myers, James; And Others **Source**: Journal of Child Language **Year**: 1996

70. What Do Parents Expect: Children's Language Acquisition in a Bilingual Community. **Author**: Aldridge, Michelle; Waddon, Alun **Source**: Language Awareness **Year**: 1995

71. Language Differentiation in Early Bilingual Development. **Author**: Genesse, Fred; And Others **Source**: Journal of Child Language **Year**: 1995

72. Early Acquisition of Verbs in Korean: A Cross-linguistic Study. **Author**: Choi, Soonja; Gopnik, Alison **Source**: Journal of Child Language **Year**: 1995

73. The Acquisition of Phonology by Cantonese-Speaking Children. **Author**: So, Lydia K. H.; Dodd, Barbara J. **Source**: Journal of Child Language **Year**: 1995

74. Syntactic Acquisition in Bilingual Children: Autonomous or Interdependent? **Author**: Paradis, Johanne; Genesse, Fred **Source**: Studies in Second Language Acquisition **Year**: 1996

75. Second versus Third Language Acquisition: Is There a Difference? **Author**: Klein, Elaine C. **Source**: Language Learning **Year**: 1995

76. The Acquisition of Tense-Aspect Morphology: A Prototype Account. **Author**: Shirai, Yasuhiro; Andersen, Roger W. **Source**: Language **Year**: 1995

77. Maturation and Learnability in Parametric Systems. **Author**: Bertolo, Stefano **Source**: Language Acquisition **Year**: 1995

78. Acquisition of French Relative Clauses Reconsidered. **Author**: Guasti, Maria Teresa **Source**: Language Acquisition **Year**: 1995

79. How Does Children's Talking Encourage the Structure of Writing? **Author**: Conlan, Kathleen **Source**: British Educational Research Journal **Year**: 1995

80. Early Lexical Acquisition and the Vocabulary Spurt: A Response to Goldfield and Reznick. **Author**: Mervis, Carolyn B.; Bertrand, Jacqueline **Source**: Journal of Child Language **Year**: 1995

81. Relative Clauses Are Barriers to "Wh"-Movement for Young Children. **Author**: De Villiers, Jill; Roeper, Thomas **Source**: Journal of Child Language **Year**: 1995

82. Bilingual Lexicon: Implications for Studies of Language Choice. **Author**: Quay, Suzanne **Source**: Journal of Child Language **Year**: 1995

83. Cross-Language Synonyms in the Lexicons of Bilingual Infants: One Language or Two? **Author**: Pearson, Barbara Zurer; And Others **Source**: Journal of Child Language **Year**: 1995

84. Early Lexical Development: The Contribution of Parental Labeling and Infants' Categorization Abilities. **Author**: Poulin-Dubois, Diane; And Others **Source**: Journal of Child Language **Year**: 1995

85. The Silenced Language of Abandoned Brazilian Children. **Author**: Kramer, Edelyn Schweidson **Source**: Rassegna Italiana di Linguistica Applicata **Year**: 1995

86. What Language Reveals about Children's Categories of Personhood. **Author**: Budwig, Nancy; Wiley, Angela **Source**: New Directions for Child Development **Year**: 1995

87. Book Reviews. **Author**: Fisher, Robert; And Others **Source**: International Journal of Early Years Education **Year**: 1995

88. Interactions between Mothers and Children Who Are Deaf. **Author**: Jamieson, Janet R. **Source**: Journal of Early Intervention **Year**: 1995

89. Strategies That Make Sense. **Author**: Lifter, Karin **Source**: Journal of Early Intervention **Year**: 1995

90. Reflections on the Origins of Directiveness: Implications for Intervention. **Author**: Girolametto, Luigi **Source**: Journal of Early Intervention **Year**: 1995

91. The Value of a Good Distinction. **Author**: Dale, Philip S. **Source**: Journal of Early Intervention **Year**: 1995

92. The Role of Directives in Early Language Intervention. **Author**: McCathren, Rebecca B.; And Others **Source**: Journal of Early Intervention **Year**: 1995

93. Book Review: Understanding Word Learning or Claiming the Ethnographic Child. **Author**: Lucariello, Joan **Source**: Cognitive Development **Year**: 1995

94. A Cross-Linguistic Study of Early Lexical Development **Author**: Caselli, Maria Cristina; And Others **Source**: Cognitive Development **Year**: 1995

95. Resumptives in the Acquisition of Relative Clauses. **Author**: Perez-Leroux, Ana Teresa **Source**: Language Acquisition **Year**: 1995

96. Questions, Relatives, and Minimal Projection. **Author**: Demuth, Katherine **Source**: Language Acquisition **Year**: 1995

97. Metrical Patterns of Words and Production Accuracy. **Author**: Schwartz, Richard G.; Goffman, Lisa **Source**: Journal of Speech and Hearing Research **Year**: 1995

98. Subjectivity in Children's Fictional Narrative. **Author**: Hewitt, Lynne E.; Duchan, Judith Felson **Source**: Topics in Language Disorders **Year**: 1995

99. The Effects of Age on the Rate of Learning a Second Language. **Author**: Slavoff, Georgina R.; Johnson, Jacqueline S. **Source**: Studies in Second Language Acquisition **Year**: 1995

100. Language Learning in Context: Teacher and Toddler Speech in Three Classroom Play Areas. **Author**: O'Brien, Marion; Bi, Xiufen **Source**: Topics in Early Childhood Special Education **Year**: 1995

101. Examination of the Stability of Two Methods of Defining Specific Language Impairment. **Author**: Cole, Kevin N.; And Others **Source**: Applied Psycholinguistics: **Year**: 1995

102. Effects of Age of Acquisition on Grammatical Sensitivity: Evidence from On-Line and Off-Line Tasks. **Author**: Emmorey, Karen; And Others **Source**: Applied Psycholinguistics **Year**: 1995

103. Negative Evidence on Negative Evidence. **Author**: Morgan, James L.; And Others **Source**: Developmental Psychology **Year**: 1995

104. Children's Understanding of Homonyms. **Author**: Backscheider, Andrea A.; Gelman, Susan A. **Source**: Journal of Child Language **Year**: 1995

105. Morphological Cues to Verb Meaning: Verb Inflections and the Initial Mapping of Verb Meanings. **Author**: Behrend, Douglas A.; And Others **Source**: Journal of Child Language **Year**: 1995

106. Visible Thought: Deaf Children's Use of Signed & Spoken Private Speech. **Author**: Jamieson, Janet R. **Source**: Sign Language Studies **Year**: 1995

107. An Intervention for Educating Child Care Personnel on Speech and Language Milestones. **Author**: Gorenflo, Carole W.; And Others **Source**: Early Child Development and Care **Year**: 1995

Notes

Notes